We lo
100u
children
every week!

A practical guide to children's work
– with Jesus as your role model

Graham Reed

kevin
mayhew

First published in 2005 by

KEVIN MAYHEW LTD
Buxhall, Stowmarket, Suffolk, IP14 3BW
E-mail: info@kevinmayhewltd.com
www.kevinmayhew.com

9 8 7 6 5 4 3 2 1 0

ISBN 1 84417 495 6
Catalogue No. 1500862

Cover design by Angela Selfe
Typesetting by Richard Weaver

Printed and bound in Great Britain

Contents

About the author

Graham was born into a missionary family in the Central African Belgium Congo (now the Democratic Republic of the Congo), and made his first response to the Gospel when he was just 4 years old. His teenage years were spent in Littlehampton where he became interested in children's work through the ministry of evangelist David Iliffe.

After completing a foundation course in art, Graham worked for five years as a graphic artist, but at the age of 22 he felt God calling him to work full-time as a children's evangelist and discipler. In 1982 he went to Moorlands Bible College to train for ministry and met Steph, his future wife, there. They worked for a year with David Iliffe as apprentices, learning the skills to become children's workers themselves. In 1985 they were employed by the Vine Evangelical Church in Sevenoaks to develop work amongst children and families. During their four years there, Graham and Steph were invited to begin a programme for 5s to 7s for Spring Harvest at Minehead, and 'Whizz Kids' was born in 1986. Now twenty years later the programme (much improved from those early days) is still running, under the banner of Children Worldwide.

In 1990 Graham and Steph moved to the Sheffield area and back into itinerant children's work. They met up with John and later Maria O'Brien who were to become close friends and partners in the ministry. Graham worked with John to develop a school assemblies ministry, visiting some 40 schools in and around Sheffield. Over the years Graham has worked in Africa, Europe and North America as a children's speaker and evangelist, and he has also remained deeply involved in his home church in Dronfield, where he now lives. In recent years the emphasis in his ministry has swung towards discipling young people, as he has become aware of the great challenge the Church faces in training up a generation for Christ in the 21st century.

Introduction

Little did I realise as I walked along the concrete pavements of the council estate I knew so well, that it was going to be one of those days that changed the direction of my life. Nothing dramatic happened, but I began to look around me at the blocks of flats. Picking up children on Sundays and Wednesdays for church activities meant that I knew the occupants of many of the flats I was looking at. Many of those families were hurting, some were falling apart, and I was surprised to find tears welling up. I felt a strong sense of God calling me to do something more than the kids' club I was trying to run with little or no experience and no training. This started me on a journey which led me to Bible school, and after a long time has brought me to the point of writing this book.

Today there are twelve million children and young people in the United Kingdom. Fewer than one million of them have a strong link with a church, and fewer than 400,000 have a personal relationship with Jesus. Each week 1000 decide not to go to church again, or drift away because they do not feel they belong.

The Church faces a huge challenge if it is to survive in the 21st century. The biggest challenge is not how to recruit new children; it is how to keep the ones we've got!

So where do we begin? First we need a God's eye view of children, then we need to understand that we have to make some radical decisions about how we do church, and how we minister to and with, young people.

To my family who have travelled with me on the journey. Steph, Dan, Faith and Esther.

Chapter 1

Jesus and Children, Disciples and Wormholes

Another day on the road with Jesus. The disciples jostle together out of earshot of the Master. The heat and dust of the midday sun matches their mood as they argue. Perhaps Peter is on his high horse again. After all, it's not every day that Jesus sends you out to hook a fish with enough money in its mouth to pay for Jesus' tax as well as your own! In the end the inevitable suggestion is made. 'Right then! Let's ask Jesus – then you'll see!'

'*Who is the greatest in the kingdom of heaven?*' they ask. The arrogance of the question is disguised for the moment by their feelings.

'Actions speak louder than words.' Jesus' whole life demonstrates the truth of this statement. Now is no exception. His eyes scan the edge of the crowd, where children dart playfully about like dragonflies. His gaze meets with the sparkling eyes of a little boy, not much older than a toddler. Gleefully abandoning his game, at Jesus' request he makes his way from the edge of the crowd to stand right in the centre, beside the Good Shepherd. He's snotty nosed, with grazed knees, not expecting to be the centre of attention. Jesus picks him up in his arms.

This simple action is enough in itself to change the mood of the disciples. Arrogance melts into embarrassment. The child grins. The disciples look for wormholes, as the Master begins his reply.

> *'I tell you the truth, unless you change and become like little children, you will never enter the kingdom of heaven. Therefore, whoever humbles himself like this child is the greatest in the kingdom of heaven. And whoever welcomes a little child like this in my name welcomes me. But if anyone causes one of these little ones who believes in me to sin, it would be better for him to have a large millstone hung around his neck and to be drowned in the depths of the sea.*
>
> *'Woe to the world because of the things that cause people to sin! Such things must come, but woe to the man through whom they come! If your hand or your foot causes you to sin, cut it off and throw it away. It is better for you to enter life maimed or crippled than to have two hands or two feet and to be thrown into eternal fire. And if your eye causes you to sin, gouge it out and throw it away. It is better for you to enter life with one eye, than to have two eyes and to be thrown into the fire of hell.*
>
> *'See that you do not look down on one of these little ones. For I tell you that their angels in heaven always see the face of my Father in heaven.*
>
> *'What do you think? If a man owns a hundred sheep, and one of them wanders away, will he not leave the ninety-nine on the hills and go to look for the one that wandered off? And if he finds it, I tell you the truth, he is happier about that one sheep, than about the ninety-nine that did not wander off. In the same way your Father in heaven is not willing that any of these little ones should be lost.'*
>
> (Matthew 18:3-14)

Sermon over. Not a long one – about two and a half minutes if you time it. But long enough to make the point. Much to the disciples' relief, Jesus moves on to a new subject and the little boy trots back to join his friends.

Jesus' words and actions so often shocked and angered the establishment because they ran against the traditions and practices of the day. He lived in a society where the pecking order was very important, and being pompous had become a real art, especially among those who were really 'important'. He was always turning things upside down – taking those at the bottom of the heap, and putting them on the top. In Jesus' day children were not important. Boys could not take part in the real life of the synagogue until they were twelve. Girls were destined to stay in the area designated for women, and any God-fearing man worth his sort would thank God daily that he had not been born a woman or a Gentile.

The disciples saw it as a part of their job to try to monitor who got closest to Jesus. A tricky job really. No platform with neatly displayed chairs for the platform party. No beefy stewards to make sure there was a gap between Jesus and his crowd. Usually no pulpit to put him six feet above contradiction. There were more than a few hairy moments! The health and safety people would have had a fit if they had seen how many people were in the house the time the paralytic was healed, especially when his friends made such a mess of the roof! Then there was that woman who touched Jesus' cloak and was healed after her long, sad illness. *'Who touched my clothes?'* Jesus asked! The disciples nearly laughed out loud! 'Who didn't touch my clothes?' might have been a better question. Peter could not forget the day his fishing boat was used as a floating pulpit. At least Jesus was safe from the crush. As long as he didn't fall overboard!

Now the last thing you want when you are having a constant struggle with the crowds is kids getting under your feet. The best thing the disciples can do is keep them out on the edge along with any old women and the odd leper. But Jesus had a habit of bringing the edge into the middle and sending the middle away.

So here we go with Jesus' wonderful two-and-a-half-minute sermon. It is mainly a lesson in humility for his disciples rather than a sermon about children, but it has within it nuggets of truth which were uncomfortably radical in Jesus' day, especially for his embarrassed disciples. It is just as uncomfortably radical for us today, as Jesus' modern-day disciples often still try to maintain order by keeping children on the edge.

Since our quest is to begin to see children through the eyes of Jesus, our look at this passage will be with that in mind. What can we learn about children, and what can we learn through children?

'I tell you the truth . . .'

Here's a little phrase Jesus used when he had something important to say. If like me you were brought up with the King James Version of the Bible, then this is a 'Verily' (always seemed a rather funny word to me as a child!). The disciples knew they were going to have to listen! No getting away.

'. . . unless you change . . .'

Jesus is about to talk to his disciples about having child-like qualities. In view of their argument, which is highlighted in Mark's account, it is not surprising that Jesus points out that the disciples need to change before they can demonstrate child-like qualities. It is not enough for the disciples to look for those child-like qualities they already have and build on them. A decision needs to be made on their part to be different. The King James Version translates Jesus' words 'Except ye be converted . . .' This implies a complete transformation. The kind of change Jesus talks about can only take place when the Holy Spirit is in control of someone's life after they have been converted.

'. . . and become like little children . . .'

The word here for 'little children' is *teknon* in the Greek. It would normally be used for children from toddler age to about five years old. It is worth noting that Jesus uses this same word throughout this passage in verses 2, 3, 4, 5, 10 and 14. It is no accident that Jesus taught his disciples about children using a very young child as his example. As we will see, what he had to say about their value and the value of their spirituality was radical in the culture in which Jesus spoke. It is equally challenging to the way we treat children, and to the way we 'do' church today. What is it about the innocence, trust and dependence of an unspoilt child that God wants us to learn to rediscover?

'. . . you will never enter the kingdom of heaven.'

Jesus isn't exactly answering the disciples' question. *'Who is the greatest?'* they had blustered, but Jesus talks about getting in. 'Unless you change and become like this little child,' Jesus explains to his red-faced followers, 'you will not even get in to the kingdom of heaven. Forget about being the greatest.' In Jesus' upside-down world, greatness is not linked to position. The great are among the most pecked rather than those who peck first. He advises his disciples to ensure *entrance* to the kingdom rather than *position* in it.

But what does this tell us about children? Something very simple, and very profound. Nobody can be more child-like than a child. 'Adults,' Jesus says, 'need to become like a child to enter the kingdom of heaven.' They need to go through a considered change. Children are already child-like. This means that they stand on the threshold of the kingdom of heaven and are better positioned to enter than any adult. Why is it then that we are so suspicious of child evangelism, and so sceptical of its fruit? How often do we hear a slightly patronising 'Mmm, that's nice' when the conversion of a child is announced – a little bit different from the angelic party in heaven we read about when Jesus tells the story of the lost sheep in Luke 15.

The great preacher Charles H. Spurgeon is reputed to have asked one of his deacons how many commitments to Jesus had been made once after he had been preaching. 'One and a half,' came the reply, 'an adult and a child.' 'You are right to say one and a half,' said Spurgeon, 'the one is the child with their whole life ahead of them, and the half is the adult.'

I thank God that my first response to the love of Jesus came when I was four years old. With my mother at my side I 'asked Jesus into my heart'. I cannot remember a time when God has not been an intimate part of my life, even though I can look back at 'prodigal patches' when I drifted away from God. I am also grateful for parents who wholeheartedly believed I could enter into the kingdom of heaven when I was so young.

Often, in our scepticism we are inclined to want to wait and see if a child's response to the gospel is borne out in the following months and years by fruit. But it is that very scepticism that provides poor soil for that tender new shoot to grow in. If we begin by taking the child's faith seriously, we are much more likely to help the young disciple to grow, and the child is less likely to be beset with doubt and disillusionment, two of the enemy's favourite tools for undoing new Christians.

'Therefore whoever humbles himself like this child is the greatest in the kingdom of heaven.'

Now at last Jesus talks about who is the greatest. It is the one who humbles himself to become like the toddler in his arms. Here is another lesson for the disciples. Oh how they wish that they had not argued. How silly their pettiness seems all of a sudden. To be great means you have to be humble. I wonder if they remember this incident a few weeks later when Jesus strips off his clothes and ties a towel around his waist in readiness to wash their parched feet.

But what does Jesus mean when he says '. . . *humble your-self like this child*'? What characteristics of humility does a child demonstrate for us to copy?

A child's identity is not based on what they do for a job, on how many qualifications they have acquired, or on how much money they are worth. It is not based on the size of their house, the model of car they drive, or how much power they have over other people These are some of the ways in which adults judge each other's value and worth. Even as Christians we can base our sense of worth on our position or ministry in the church. If you ask a child who she is, she will not tell you she is an accountant or a dinner lady, she will probably tell you her name. Children have not had time to build up around them all the things that the world values. They are 'naked' of all these things, and with that nakedness comes humility. It is this kind of humility that God loves.

Secondly, children demonstrate humility in their ability to receive. I am glad to say that the illustration I am about to use is still true today, though I have been using it for a number of years. Soon after moving to Dronfield, we discovered a very nice play area called Cliff Park, which has seats for weary parents, and a patio with a kiosk selling drinks, sweets and ice creams. Over the years when our children were young we made many dozens of trips there. Part of the ritual of going to the park for the children was to ask for an ice cream. It did not matter if it was summer or winter, it was always worth a try. Sometimes the harassed parent obliged, and sometimes we said no, but they always asked. There was no sense of embarrassment about asking, and I can truthfully say that they never said, 'Dad, put your wallet away, we're paying for the ice creams today. What would you like?' Somehow they got it into their heads that our relationship made it alright for them to ask and receive with no thought of having to pay for it themselves – just because I'm their dad, and they are my children.

This is exactly how God wants us to receive from him. There is nothing I can do to earn my salvation. Payment has been arranged by my heavenly Father. All I have to do is ask for it, and receive it. The same goes for God's grace, forgiveness and mercy, and a million and one blessings that he has in mind for me.

As adults we find it so hard to accept something for nothing. We would prefer to pay for our own ice cream, and everyone else's too. It makes us feel important. We would all have eternal life lined up with our life assurance policy and our pension if all we had to do was buy it, but no, God doesn't want us to buy it; it's free but, to receive it, he wants us to humble ourselves, and that's much harder.

Hudson Pope once said: 'The gateway into the kingdom of heaven is three feet high.' Children can walk straight in, but adults have to stoop. Men seem to do more to build up worldly systems of value around them than women do. Is that why there are so many more women committed to following Jesus than there are men, in western cultures? How old will we let the new generation of young men get before we treat their need for salvation seriously?

Jesus commends people who humble themselves. This does not have to do with inherited character, but a deliberate choice. It is part of the process of becoming like a child.

Jesus recognises that children still carry a humility which God attaches greatness to. Let us be careful in our desire to see children quickly reach spiritual maturity, not to rob them of their childhood and the humbleness so valued by Jesus.

'And whoever welcomes a little child like this in my name welcomes me.'

What is it about Sunday mornings? I know Sunday is supposed to be a day of rest and worship, but the rest bit often seems to be missing. It is as if the enemy gets up extra early and has a big breakfast to fortify himself for the rigours of a busy day. He is particularly keen to try and hassle families preparing to set off for a meeting, or preachers getting ready to preach. I remember one Sunday morning when I was supposed to be taking a meeting somewhere. The car has developed a habit of not starting, and since it is Sunday morning the enemy has made a special effort to make sure that everything under the bonnet is damp. I have just finished a session with Steph's hairdryer on the plugs, and at last the engine grudgingly begins to turn over. I am late. My hands are covered in oil. My clean shirt is sweaty. I am off to preach and I am not full of the joy of the Lord. I turn to look over my left shoulder to back out of the drive and there is a tap on the driver's window. Two smartly dressed men in suits with large Bibles tucked under their arms stand with gleaming white smiles right by the driver's door. Somehow I know these are not angels sent to help me in my hour of need, and no, I do not want a copy of *The Watchtower*! To back out I must turn sharply. To do this will force my two visitors onto a muddy flowerbed. I am sorely tempted, but with hindsight I am pleased that I waited for them to get off the drive before backing out. All the way to my meeting my conscience reminds me that Jesus loves the two men I have just been so rude to. I don't remember how the meeting went.

If you work with children on Sunday morning things can be even more stressful. There is the chicken to stuff and the timer to set on the oven, your visual aids to complete and find, a room to set out, and a whole load of junk that someone else has left in there! Just when you begin to breathe again, the children come flooding in like a little tidal wave, full of energy and letting off the steam that has been building to a head during the hymn sandwich or forty-minute float away session they have just experienced. Of course it does not need to be like this, but the enemy likes it to be like this. If there is one thing the enemy does not like, it is the word of God, so you might like to remind him of this verse the next time you feel stressed at the beginning of your Sunday group. 'Whoever welcomes a little child like this in my name welcomes me.'

This is a verse I don't fully understand. Some of its meaning is a mystery. Perhaps some Scripture is supposed to be that way. But one thing is clear from this wonderful statement. Children are extremely precious to Jesus. The phrase *'in my name'* could be translated 'for my sake'. How important it is each time we meet together to seek the presence of Jesus, and oh, how we long for him to reveal himself to us. Stoop and welcome a little child as she comes in and Jesus puts this on a level with welcoming him.

This little phrase is a wonderful encouragement for anyone involved in children's ministry. Jesus doesn't only value children. He values those who value them. Welcoming Jesus is so central to our worship. It is something that happens in the middle of our times of worship. Many children's workers feel that they are on the edge of what is going on. They often feel far more marginalised than the children whom they work with. Here Jesus puts children's ministry into context – right at the heart of Jesus himself.

To welcome is not to teach. Our main calling when we are serving Jesus among children is to build a loving relationship with them. This comes above what we can teach. To welcome is to make someone feel loved and valued. To let them know that we are pleased that they are in our presence. This can be a challenge. Some children are much more endearing than others.

Yes, it is true that you never forget a good teacher. It is also true that children do not forget a good Sunday Group leader. Each child in your class will remember you in thirty years' time. They may not be able to identify the details of any specific lesson you taught them, but they will remember you. They will be able to recount their impression of you as a person. Who we are, our attitudes, values and character speak louder than the contents of our lesson, or the application to our Bible story.

In the midweek club I run called Kool Kids, I always try to catch each child as they come in and address them personally by name. Individual attention is just a little way of welcoming in the name of Jesus.

'But if anyone causes one of these little ones who believe in me to sin . . .'

Two new words have arrived: Believe, and Sin.

Jesus begins to issue a warning, but as he does so it is important to note that now Jesus is talking about believing children.

First we must note that children can believe. Belief and faith are very closely allied as the writer to the Hebrews points out in chapter 11 verse 1: *'Now faith is being sure of what we hope for and certain of what we do not see.'*

I do not know too many five-year-old atheists. Children find it easy to believe in God, miracles and the supernatural. It was always something precious to spend those few minutes with our children before the lights were put out and the final goodnight said. Bedtime prayers became intimate chats with God. When they were young they never questioned God's existence, even though they could not see him. They have always known that God is part of our family. Belief for them was completely natural. Their faith was very strong. It was based on the simple premise that God is here, he cares for us and is strong enough to look after us. I know these things are true, but my adult mind mixes belief with doubt every time I come to tackle some issue that demands faith.

Children find it much easier to pray for healing, for example, because their faith is far less cluttered with doubt. I highly recommend that any prayer-for-healing team includes believing children.

Jesus affirms that little children can sin. One reason that there is a lack of urgency about child evangelism is that many people do not believe that children can sin, or that somehow when a child sins it does not carry the same consequences as it does for an adult. Romans 3:23 reminds us that *'All have sinned and fall short of the glory of God,'* and Romans 6:23 says, *'the wages of sin is death.'* The consequence of sin on a child's life is deadly, just as it is for an adult. Jesus goes on to reinforce the seriousness of this in the verses that follow.

'. . . it would be better for him to have a large millstone hung around his neck and to be drowned in the depths of the sea.'

Up in the Derbyshire Peak District near to where we live there are quarries where in years gone by millstone grit has been hacked out and shaped into what look like giant Polo mints three to four feet across. They were used in Sheffield, and further afield where water turned them to grind steel. Some that are not quite perfect have been left where they were cut, a fascinating reminder of the past. Not many have been used for suicidal drownings recently, yet whenever I see them, I remember this verse. If you did tie one round your neck and jump into the sea, your descent would be very rapid, and your end very certain.

The warning here is to anyone who causes believing children to sin, and the recommended consequences may not have been intended literally, but they do underline the gravity of what Jesus is saying.

So to whom is this passage speaking? Is it a warning to child abusers, or potential child abusers? Yes, perhaps it is. Whenever another harrowing story of a murdered or abused child bursts out of the television set, my mind wanders back to this passage. These stories are so frequent now that I can sit through the news and they hardly touch me unless I begin to think about what has really happened. God does not become immune to these stories like I do. The full horror of them reaches deep into his heart. The difference is that I was not there when that child was murdered or raped, but God *was* there. He experienced the full horror of it, and he is a God of justice.

The sense of indignation, anger and pain felt by any parent when their child is abused, reflects the way God feels when a child is mistreated. There is a warning here not to mess with children because they are immensely precious to God.

First of all, though, this is a warning to anyone who will not take the faith of a child seriously. It is no accident that Jesus has used the word 'believes' here. The *belief* of a child is so precious to God that woe betide anyone who leads that child off the rails so that they sin.

There are two ways that this can happen.

Close one eye for a moment so that you can use your imagination. (Keep the other open so that you can read!)

You are a leader on a children's camp. You have been asked to lead a night ramble through the woods. You are supplied with the only torch, and so you set out at the front. Another leader trails along at the back of the group, but they must rely on moonlight! (I don't recommend you actually do this!) Off you go with your trusting group of excited children. Sadly, as you walk through the woods the power goes to your head, and you set about tripping the children up! Whenever you get the chance you pull a dead branch out of the woods, across the path. Shining your torch well ahead, you carefully step over the branch yourself but your trusting followers all trip over the branch and fall flat on their faces.

You can open both eyes for a few moments to think!

This is a parable of someone who deliberately sets out to cause children to sin. There are plenty of dead branches lying around today, and it would be easy to teach our believing children to sin! But nobody (I hope) in their right mind would do such a thing.

Now close the other eye and imagine again.

The scene is exactly as before. Yes, for some reason they have trusted you with the torch again! This time there is a difference. With exemplary self-control you manage to resist the temptation to drag branches out of the bushes. This time there is no need to. As you shine your torch along the path ahead you can see that there are loads of branches already strewn across your route. Carefully noting where each branch lies you pick your way over each obstacle but you say nothing to those following you and you always keep the torch shining well ahead. The effect is exactly the same as in the first scenario. The children all trip over and fall flat on their faces!

Both eyes open? Good. The question then, is when were you most to blame – when you pulled the branches out or when you failed to shine the light on the branches that were already there? Arguably both are equally damaging.

We know that as children's leaders, whether at home as parents, or as kids' workers in our local church setting, our job is not to knowingly cause children to sin. Much more often we are guilty of not helping our children to avoid the stumbling blocks that are already there.

Over the years fashions and crazes come and go that affect our children. Many are harmless, but others have ungodly or even occultic influences imbedded in them. Over recent years Pokemon and – much longer lasting – Harry Potter have raised serious concerns among many parents and children's workers, including myself!

There are other perennial stumbling blocks, which have been there for a long time. The only way they change is that they seem to trip children up younger than ever before. The whole area of sex and relationships is a good example of this. Unless our children have a good biblical foundation laid for them by the time they leave primary school, that foundation will be laid for them by their peers in the first few weeks of secondary school, and in most cases their values are not biblical. This does not mean that we need to sit our children down and read them a list of rules to follow. We need to help our children understand what the Bible says, but we also need to help them understand some of the pressures they are going to face, and plan with them how they are going to cope. The Christian life is a challenge and an adventure not a prison.

The WWJD culture which Christian children and young people are adopting is a great way of helping them to begin to think about some of the pitfalls for themselves, but along with wearing the bracelet, there needs to be good, open and realistic teaching about all the issues that our young people are facing today, and practical discussions on how to make godly decisions about what to say, do and see.

A few years ago I visited the States for a Children's Ministry conference. One of the things that struck those of us who went was the very strong code of discipline operated by the host church with their young people. They did not allow believing young people in early and middle teens to date, because they felt the temptation for them to get involved in a physical relationship was too strong for them. If a relationship developed someone would talk to him or her gently and firmly and ask them to break it off. To some this will seem like legalism, but the church there had many hundreds of radiant, committed Christian young people who loved their youth leader, and appreciated the fact that they did not have to been seen to have a girlfriend or boyfriend in order to fit in with their friends. The key was the loving, serving relationship that had been built up between leader and young people, so the yoke was not heavy or legalistic in its application.

Materialism is one of the biggest gods of western society. It is a huge stumbling block for believing children. Here children are looking at us for example. What we demonstrate will have a bigger impact than what we teach. How important to us and our sense of self worth are the things we own? Do we hold them lightly? Are we prepared to lend them? Does my car say who I am? Do I need to wear designer labels? Is the direction of my life dictated by how much I will earn? This is an example of an area where our own values will say more to the young people we work with than the Bible lesson we teach.

We could go on. The list of 'branches' is endless. The important thing is that we are always on the lookout for those that are relevant to our children now. You won't pull them off the path by yourself – some of them are too heavy. Ask your children to help you and do it together.

For those of us who are parents or children's leaders there is a challenge here to recognise that prevention is better than cure. So much time is spent in youth work trying to repair the damage already done through sin, because children have not seen the light of God shone on the issues that start to tug at them while they are still in primary school, or even before.

'Woe to the world because of the things that cause people to sin! Such things must come, but woe to the man through whom they come! If your hand or your foot causes you to sin, cut it off and throw it away. It is better for you to enter life maimed or crippled than to have two hands or two feet and to be thrown into eternal fire. And if your eye causes you to sin, gouge it out and throw it away. It is better for you to enter life with one eye, than to have two eyes and to be thrown into the fire of hell.'

Once more Jesus warns about the source of sinful practice. This is a warning for each of us as individuals to cut ourselves off from the tools that enable us to sin. It is also a warning to root out anyone who could be a sinful influence on children.

It is notable that Jesus uses the hand, the foot and the eye as examples of tools of sinful behaviour. In our culture, too many children are abused at the hands of adults, as we shall see in the next chapter. With child pornography more accessible than ever, the eye is also used for ungodly practice.

Sadly the church is not immune to these problems, and today more than ever before we need to make sure that what we do is righteous, and what we are seen to do is righteous. With this in mind there are a number of safeguards, which will help to ensure good practice:

1. All children's workers should fill in an application to work with children, which should include a declaration about any criminal convictions, past or pending.

2. All children's workers should be referenced, including at least one reference from a church leader.

3. Every church should have a simple good practice guide, which every children's worker should be familiar with. Children's workers should never be on their own with children.

4. Every church should make known the name and phone number of a person they can call in confidence should a problem arise. This should be someone in the church with authority, but not necessarily directly involved in the children's work.

5. All those working with children in the church should be police checked.

Even with the best good practice procedures in place, things can and do still go wrong. It is vital that we look out for each other, and do not let suspicious behaviour go unchecked. On the one hand vigilance helps to protect our children, and on the other it helps us to protect our team of children's workers from false allegations.

The Churches' Child Protection Advisory Service (CCPAS) provides excellent training and resources to churches who want to make sure that their children's work is being carried out to the highest standard of safety. They also provide support and advice for churches who find they have to deal with a case of abuse.

'See that you do not look down on one of these little ones . . .'

The disciples didn't know which way to look. They were probably still literally looking down, knowing they could not leave until Jesus had finished, and still feeling rather embarrassed!

What Jesus is really saying is, 'Don't patronise children,' or 'Don't underestimate their value.'

We have already touched on one area where we patronise children – that is when we don't take their 'belief' seriously. What are some of the other ways in which we are in danger of looking down on children?

Being patronising can sometimes be subtle and unintentional. I was leading an all-age service one Education Sunday and asked for children to come and pray for their school. Over the years I have found that there is one age group that will volunteer for anything. They will volunteer before they even know what you want. These are Key Stage One children aged four to seven. I had four helpful volunteers, and each one prayed simply and clearly for their school. After the last one had finished there was a brief pause and then everyone clapped. Nobody would have clapped if adults had said the prayers. The intention was to show appreciation and encouragement, but along with that came the message that what had just happened was some kind of a performance, and therefore not the real thing.

There is a place for performance. No Christmas is complete without that Nativity play, and children learn a great deal from performing. They gain confidence to speak in public, they learn to use their voices and work as part of a team. Performance can also make a valuable contribution to the content of a service by presenting a story or bringing an application to life. But if the only way children can express themselves in meetings is through performance, then we are in danger of not taking their relationship with God seriously, and then we go against the words of Jesus when he said, *'Do not look down on one of these little ones.'*

The prayer meeting is sinking into a numb depression. Nobody can find the words to lift it. Prayers seem to drift aimlessly towards the ceiling before floating downwards to rest heavily on the floor – and then a child prays. Most of us have been at that prayer meeting and know the effect that child has. It is not just because it is 'nice'. There is something in it that really lifts the spirit and the whole atmosphere changes.

Usually in an all-age meeting we will plan space for some kind of corporate response to the theme or message of the day. On one Sunday 'Listening to God' was our theme. We played some music and prayed that God would speak to us all individually. Everyone had a piece of paper and something to write or draw with. Minutes later one or two people shared what they felt God was saying or showing them. An eight-year-old boy had a picture of a beach. The tide was coming in. Halfway up the beach was a huge hole, deep and empty. When I asked him what he felt the picture was about, he said he didn't know. For the previous year or so we had been praying as a church for revival. Specifically we had prayed that God would use our town, even our building, as a well of revival.

This picture seemed to fit in with that idea, and it was a great encouragement to me to pray on.

On another occasion I was waiting to go forward to speak. My heart was full of what I felt God wanted me to say, and a child came up beside me and quietly asked me if I wanted prayer before I preached. I began to cry as the child prayed, and I don't think I stopped until the service was over. I can't remember a more exhausting preach! Many dads were deeply affected by what God was saying that day.

One last little story of how children can minister.

Our family has been involved in Christian work for a number of years in Latvia. One year we were invited to work at a camp way out in the forest. Conditions were very basic and we had lots of adventures, but that's another story! When we got there, the interpreter we applied for did not materialise, so for the first few days our interpreter was a thirteen-year-old girl. She interpreted all our conversations and my talks at the morning and evening meetings. That was a ministry in itself. During the week we got to know a girl whom I will call Vanessa. She was ten years old and though her first language was Russian, she spoke quite good English. She had a younger brother whom I will call Aldin. Vanessa and Aldin came from a very poor family. Their parents were both deaf and both were alcoholics, so Vanessa often found herself looking after the needs of her whole family. At the end of the week we received a beautifully decorated invitation to have supper with Vanessa and the other children and leader from her tent. These supper visits were important occasions. Gifts would be exchanged and we would share polite conversation. We took Liquorice Allsorts as a gift from our home city of Sheffield. The children brought wild strawberries plaited onto necklaces and sweet-scented wild flowers. We were asked to share our testimonies, and to answer questions about Jesus. We were also asked to pray a blessing on each child. At the end, when our gifts were finally exchanged, Vanessa brought out a small cuddly Snoopy dog, which she handed over with obvious affection. 'This is my only toy,' she said, 'and I give it to you because I love you.'

Later, as I was thinking about this, I was reminded of John 3:16, the best-known verse in the whole Bible, which says, *'God loved the world so much that he gave his only Son.'* Vanessa's gift was precious because it was her only toy. Now, through the loving action of a ten-year-old girl, I have a much deeper appreciation of an old verse gone stale with familiarity.

Something powerful happens when we begin to take the spiritual contribution of children seriously. In a way we stop looking down on them and begin to look straight into their faces – on the level. One consequence of this, as I have tried to show with these little stories, is that children can and do begin to minister in the body of the church. This helps their faith to grow, but it also blesses me, and the rest of the church. Here is a resource that we are in danger of disabling by not taking its value seriously.

'For I tell you that their angels in heaven always see the face of my Father in heaven.'

Here is another remarkable verse relating to believing children. The words 'their angels' implies that each believing child has one or more angels appointed to them. This verse tells us that there is an intimate link between the child's angel and the Father himself, into whose face they gaze.

On many occasions when my children have been afraid, particularly at night, I have reminded them of this verse. 'Don't forget you have an angel, and they can see God's face.'

This idea of believers having angels appointed to serve and protect them is backed up in other parts of Scripture. In Psalm 34:7 David wrote these words when he was in a very frightening situation: *'The angel of the Lord encamps around those who fear him, and he delivers them.'*

The Bible has a lot to say about angels, and it can be a great encouragement for children to know about them. The problem is, that most children think angels are overgrown fairies, taking their picture of what an angel is like from last year's Christmas cards rather than the Bible. Who wants to be protected by a floaty, effeminate wisp with a Readybrek glow?

Daniel chapter 10 paints a much more exciting picture of what angels are like: *'I looked up and there before me was a man dressed in linen, with a belt of the finest gold around his waist. His body was like chrysolite, his face like lightning, his eyes like flaming torches, his arms and legs like the gleam of burnished bronze, and his voice like the sound of a multitude.*

'I, Daniel was the only one who saw the vision; the men with me did not see it, but such terror overwhelmed them that they fled and hid themselves. So I was left alone, gazing at this great vision; I had no strength left, my face turned deathly pale and I was helpless.'

Now if this guy were sent to protect me, I really would feel protected! As the story goes on we are given a little glimpse of the ministry of this gladiator angel, as he explains to Daniel why he is late!

'Then he continued: "Do not be afraid Daniel. Since the first day that you set your mind to gain understanding, and to humble yourself before your God (now there's a little phrase we've seen before!) *your words were heard, and I have come in response to them. But the prince of the Persian kingdom resisted me twenty-one days. Then Michael, one of the chief princes, came to help me, because I was detained there with the king of Persia. Now I have come to explain to you what will happen to your people in the future".'*

This angel is part of the army of the Lord, fighting in one of the great spiritual battles that we are so often unaware of, but he is also a messenger. All this paints a rather different picture in my imagination from the glowing Christmas card. Why not read this passage to your children and ask them to draw what they think the angel looked like!

Hebrews 1:14 gives us another glimpse into the ministry of angels: *'Are not all angels ministering spirits sent to serve those who will inherit salvation?'*

The child's angel does not just form a passive link between the child and God, they have a part in ministering to the believer.

There were at least two occasions when angels carried out this role in the life of Jesus. First, during the time of Jesus' temptations in the desert. Forty days' fasting had left Jesus exhausted. Satan knew the best time to strike. Jesus had a test to face, but the angels were standing by to minister to him at the Father's command: *'Then the devil left him, and angels came and attended him'* (Matthew 4:11).

In Gethsemane Jesus faced another huge test, as he pleaded with his Father to take the cup from him, and then reaffirmed his commitment to do the Father's will: *'An angel from heaven appeared to him, and strengthened him'* (Luke 22:43).

I don't know if angels appointed to believing children cease to function in that capacity when the child becomes an adult. I rather hope not, but I do know that we can teach our children that God uses angels to minister to them.

In recent years I have become increasingly aware of stories children and adults have told me of angelic encounters. One boy told me about waking up in the night to see a powerful figure glowing with light in his room. Although he was only about nine years old, he said he did not feel in the least bit afraid.

A dad told me how he had gone in late at night to check that his sleeping infant was OK. On entering the room he saw what he believes was an angel in the corner of the room overlooking the child. This incident reminded him of a similar experience he recalled from his own childhood.

A mum told me how having lost her first baby at only a few days old, she had clearly been visited by an angel who had brought a sense of comfort to her.

'What do you think? If a man owns a hundred sheep, and one of them wanders away, will he not leave the ninety-nine on the hills and go to look for the one that wandered off?'

Like any good preacher, Jesus probably used his parables on more than one occasion. When we read the story of the lost sheep in Luke's Gospel, it is told in a different context. There, Jesus wanted the Pharisees to understand that he had come to find lost sinners, and this was the reason he spent time with them.

In Matthew's Gospel the story is told directly in the context of children. We know this because in Jesus' summary in Matthew 18:14 he says, *'In the same way your Father in heaven is not willing that any of these little ones should be lost.'*

Looking after sheep in Jesus' day was a little different from today. Usually English sheep are left to their own devices, whether in a carefully fenced field, or out on the hills. The farmer will round them up if they need to be moved, dipped or sheared. Shepherds in Israel became very well acquainted with their sheep. They practically lived with them. During the day they were allowed to graze under the watchful eye of the shepherd, who was always on the lookout for wild animals that might come and worry the flock. At night they were herded into a rough stone enclosure and the shepherd himself would lie across the entrance to the fold, making sure no undesirables got in, and no sheep got out. It would be common practice to count in all your sheep each night to make sure none was lost, like a Sunday school teacher counting the children back onto the coach at the end of a day's outing.

This is the setting to Jesus' parable. The shepherd has become aware that he is missing a sheep, so he risks everything, leaving the main flock grazing on the hillside or tucked up in the fold, to search for the one lost sheep. In John 10:11 Jesus says, *'I am the good shepherd. The good shepherd lays down his life for the sheep.'*

Bearing in mind that in this case the sheep are little children, we have a wonderful picture of Jesus searching for children who are spiritually lost. From the world's perspective this shepherd may have been considered unwise. 'The needs of the many outweigh the needs of the individual,' one might logically say. 'The shepherd should have left the lost sheep for fear of harm coming to the rest of the flock.' But Jesus is intimately concerned for the individual.

Our towns and cities are full of lost sheep today. Statistics suggest that as many as one in ten children suffer from physical, emotional or sexual abuse. That's over a million children in the UK. The Good Shepherd's heart breaks for each individual case. He is there when they suffer, and knows each thought and feeling in their young hearts and minds. Fewer than one in twenty children ever get the chance to find out about the real Jesus through belonging to a church.

Here's another thought. Since Paul teaches us that we are the body of Christ, and since another name for Christ is the Good Shepherd, that makes us the body of the Good Shepherd! If it is the Good Shepherd's strong desire to go and search for lost sheep, then we should follow his example. Before noting one or two things the Good Shepherd didn't do, it is worth spotting a couple of things about our lost sheep.

1. He wandered away and got lost

While children are little they can wander away from God. When this happens they become spiritually lost, and vulnerable to the enemy.

31

The word 'wander' is a good one to describe what happens to children. As we have already seen, there is something built into every child that makes it easy for them to believe in God. People wander away from God when they face away from him and begin to move. This happens as their attitudes and values are eroded by those around them. As they begin to think, say and do what is against God's will it is as if sin takes them by the hand, and gently leads them further and further away from the fold. 'Wander' implies a gradual process rather than a dramatic instantaneous decision. It is the process by which we lose many hundreds of children and young people from the church every year.

The writer to the Hebrews, aware of this possibility, warns his readers to be careful not to become lost sheep: *'We must pay more careful attention, therefore, to what we have heard, so that we do not drift away'* (Hebrews 2:1).

2. He was found and brought back

While children are little they can be found by the Good Shepherd, and brought home (Luke 15:5). In Luke's account there is a close link between this story and the story of the lost son who followed the same pattern of misadventure.

In both cases the main character starts in a safe place but wanders away. In both cases the character finds themselves in need of rescue. In both cases they are loved and valued by the one they wander away from, and in both cases there is rejoicing on their return!

Three things the Good Shepherd didn't do:

- Noticing the lost sheep was missing, he realised that he was only a lamb and therefore could not get properly lost.

- Finding the lost sheep he realised that he was only a lamb and so left him in the gorse bush until he was old enough to understand how he could be rescued.

- Returning the lost lamb to the fold, he did not make too much of a fuss since you can never be sure whether a lamb of that age has really been found.

A little bit cynical, I know, but I'm sure you get the point.

Leaving Capernaum for a few minutes, let's fly off in our time machine to the beach a little further around Lake Galilee. It is early morning and the disciples have enjoyed a great cooked breakfast. Peter wanders along the shore with Jesus who asks him three times. *'Simon son of John, do you truly love me?'* (John 21). Peter's heart is full of shame and sadness. He knows the circumstances that have led Jesus to ask him. Each time Peter reaffirms his love for the Lord Jesus, the Good Shepherd commissions him to feed or care for his sheep. Well, not quite each time. After Peter's first *'Yes Lord, you know that I love you,'* Jesus says, *'Feed my lambs.'* Note: lambs *not* sheep. Traditionally the church was built on Peter the rock, who himself became one of the great Christian martyrs. Was Jesus commissioning Peter to include children in his pastoral ministry, and is this commission to the church and not just Peter?

'And if he finds it, I tell you the truth, he is happier about that one sheep, than about the ninety-nine that did not wander off.'

Everybody has got a story about getting lost. My first real experience of this was on Bournemouth beach when our family had returned to England for a year from Central Africa, where my parents were missionaries. Africa was my real home as a child. It was a classic situation. Child is left outside toilet with strict instructions not to move. Father comes out of one door thinking child is with mother. Mother comes out of another door thinking child is with Father. Child having not been collected by either parent begins to cry. An excellent tactic when lost. Friendly policeman comes up to child and asks what the problem is. Child sobs 'I'm lost!' 'Never mind, sonny' the policeman says. 'Where do you live?' 'In the Congo,' comes the helpful reply. Sensing that another line of questioning may be more fruitful, the persevering policeman asks, 'What kind of car does your father have?' 'I don't know,' the child sobs, 'but it has a tiger in its tank!' Just then flustered parent comes to retrieve child much to the relief of the bewildered policeman. (I know this story betrays my age somewhat, as the younger reader may not recognise the reference to having a 'tiger' in its tank. During the 1960s Esso had an advertising campaign for petrol using this phrase. Many drivers even had a tiger's tail attached to the petrol cap of their car to show that they did indeed have a tiger in their tank. Thankfully the kind policeman understood all this!)

Being lost is not a pleasant experience for the lost person, but it can be equally terrifying for the person who has lost someone, especially if the lost person is a little child. I will never forget losing our Hannah, when she was about two years old, in Sevenoaks market. She was only gone for about four minutes, but it was long enough for both parents to go frantic. Every story of every abducted child you have ever seen rushes headlong through your memory. Sheer panic sets in, and you want everyone to stop what they are doing until your child is found.

I wonder how our heavenly Father feels about a generation of lost children, many of whom suffer at the hands of adults.

Matthew 18:13 tells us something about the joy of the Good Shepherd when a child is brought back into relationship with him.

'In the same way your Father in heaven is not willing that any of these little ones should be lost.'

Jesus rounds up his sermon with this wonderful summary before the child in his arms is put onto the ground and runs away to play with his friends.

God's heart breaks for every child outside the fold. The one million lost children in the UK live in a secular society where behaviour and values are deteriorating. What does it mean to be lost in the twenty-first century, in the UK?

Chapter 2

The Lost Generation

Dappled sunlight filtered through the tree overhead onto an ageing wooden picnic table. The shade gave a little relief from the hot summer sun. It was July 1997 and I was speaker at a boy's camp fifty miles north of Chicago. This was a week I would remember for a lifetime, for the number of children wanting to get right with God, and for the obvious power of God at work in rough, tough Chicago boys' lives. I was getting over the culture shock. On Independence Day the leaders had explained that there was no need to be afraid of any loud bangs, as these would only be fireworks, not the small arms fire that some of them had become familiar with. One boy had seen his father die in a shooting incident, and another had been at the top of the slide in his local park in the middle of a shoot-out. He was too frightened to come down. During the week I spent many hours listening, crying, talking and praying with boys who wanted to 'get saved'. This is part of the entry for my diary on the 11 July 1997:

> One small boy aged ten gave his life to Christ today. His name was Luke. When I had finished praying with him he just put his chin on the table, looked straight at me and sighed. He looked so sad. I had been talking about God as a Father, so I asked him if he knew his dad. 'Yes,' he said, 'I met him once at a gas station.' 'What about your mom?' I asked. 'She's supposed to visit me on

Thursdays.' Later I spoke to Randy, a worker at the foster home, and found out that Luke's mother is a drug addict. She had 'forgotten' to visit the last five weeks.

When we talk about a lost generation, it sounds like a huge crowd of carefully sorted people, massed into some giant pigeonhole. God always deals with people as individuals, even when there are a lot of them. His sadness is multiplied by each Luke or Gemma, not dulled by statistics or numbers like ours.

As we take a brief look at some of the trends that affect children in our society in the UK, let's remember that we are looking at tens of thousands of individual children and families facing hardship and personal tragedy. David wrote these words when he himself was in a desperate situation: *'The Lord is close to the broken-hearted'* (Psalm 34:18). My prayer is that we will start to have a God's eye view on what is going on.

Before you go completely down the tubes though, let's also remember that we have a message of hope and restoration. The following is aimed at sharpening our awareness of the need so that we are more determined to be good news among the children who live around us.

Paul wrote: *'Remember that at that time you were separate from Christ, excluded from citizenship in Israel and foreigners to the covenants of the promise, without hope and without God in the world. But now in Christ Jesus you who once were far away have been brought near through the blood of Christ'* (Ephesians 2:12-13).

There is a hopelessness that comes from being lost, but hope is restored when people are brought near to God.

Isaiah wrote these wonderful words as he prophesied the coming Messiah. Words that were later read by Jesus himself:

> *'The Spirit of the Sovereign Lord is on me,*
> *because the Lord has anointed me*
> *to preach good news to the poor.*

He has sent me to bind up the broken-hearted,
to proclaim freedom for the captives
and release for the prisoners,
to proclaim the year of the Lord's favour
and the day of vengeance of our God,
to comfort all who mourn,
and provide for those who grieve in Zion.'
(Isaiah 61:1-3; Luke 4:18-21)

Children of the new millennium

The life of a child born in Britain in 2000 is dramatically different from that of children born in 1900. They are 'better off'. They live in a bigger house, have more toys, a better chance of a good education and much more choice when it comes to eating. They are better looked after by the State. If they are ill they get much better health care and dentistry. Inoculations free them from diseases that sometimes killed children 100 years ago. But there is another side to the coin. Children today have a much better chance of seeing their family fall apart before they are sixteen. They are more likely to get dragged into the world of drugs and to have sex while they are under age. They have a much greater chance of their life being terminated before they are born. And they are far less likely to know about Jesus.

What are some of the trends that affect children today?

This is not supposed to be a comprehensive study of society, but a snapshot of the world our children are growing up in. I am indebted to David Iliffe who has collected facts and figures for over a decade from a wide number of sources. These form the foundation for the following comments, along with statistics from Christian Research.

Family

The definition of family has changed over the last forty years. It used to mean a mother and father living with children, and

39

the phrase 'extended family' was used to bring in grandparents, uncles and aunts, cousins and other close relatives. Today the word 'family' is becoming politically incorrect, with a move towards using the word 'household'. If you ask five different people what a family is today you will probably get five different answers. This vagueness about what your family is, and who is committed to whom, creates anxiety, insecurity and worry for children.

Here are some facts relating to family in the UK:

- There are more than one and a half million single-parent families.

- More than a third of all marriages end in divorce.

- The average duration for a marriage is ten years.

- Nearly 10 per cent of married couples file for divorce within twelve months of getting married.

- England and Wales have a higher divorce rate than any other country in Europe.

- One in five children can expect their parents to divorce by the time they are sixteen.

- More than half of all divorces involve children under sixteen.

- Most children of divorced parents lose touch with their fathers within two years.

- One in twelve children live with one parent. The great majority with their mother.

Traditional family life is under threat and our children experience more pressure than ever in the shadow of the breakdown of family life.

Increasingly we live in a society where mothers have to do more to bring up children, and fathers are doing less. This is true because dads who leave home so often lose touch with their children, even though fathers who live at home with their children are more involved in things like changing nappies, taking the baby for a walk, and cooking.

One of the saddest things about the new generation is that so many children are growing up with little or no concept of having a father. This is compounded by the fact that outside the home young children are rarely cared for by a man. They may live with Mum, go to a nursery that is completely run by women, and go all the way through primary education without being taught by a man. Boys growing up in this world have no role model but the TV cartoon, pop group or sports star. Girls can grow up without knowing how to relate to men.

Men are wary about getting involved in work with children because they are afraid of being suspected of being paedophiles. Employers are often reluctant to hire men to work with children for the same reason. Yet there is a need for children to experience appropriate love and care from men in their lives if they are to develop the ability to relate to men, and in the case of boys to have real live role models to learn from, and not just the football player or pop star they see on the screen who may or may not set a good example.

What proportion of your children's team are men?

The other side of the coin is that the church has at times treated single-parent families as inferior and 'dysfunctional'. Anyone who aims to care for a family while at the same time juggling with all the other necessities of life deserves the church's encouragement and admiration! I am often reminded that God is a single-parent family, with all the attributes of a perfect father and a perfect mother. He is able to equip and help single parents for the job.

Sex, pregnancy and abortion

- The average age for loss of virginity in the UK is fifteen years and seven months, the lowest in Europe.

- More than a third of all births take place outside of marriage.
- Between 35 per cent and 40 per cent of all conceptions are aborted.
- Over five million abortions have been performed since the 1967 Abortion Act was passed.
- Half of all teenage conceptions are aborted.

These figures run alongside a drift away from strong moral absolutes, and a comparison with earlier years confirms this. For example, in 1968 there were a total of 22,256 abortions in England and Wales. In 1978 there were 142,344, and in 1996, 177,225. The number of births outside of marriage has more than doubled in the last ten years.

How does this affect people, and particularly children? Peer pressure tries to force children into conforming. Whereas it used to be the exception to have sex while you were still at school, it is now the 'norm'. Teenagers seeking an abortion were treated with shameful disdain forty years ago, leaving many cut off from friends and family; now the pendulum has swung the other way, and abortion can be a simple solution for an inconvenience. The reality is that abortion is not a simple solution. It leaves in its wake huge psychological problems for the young people concerned, which can affect them emotionally and spoil any future relationships they have.

Sex education emphasises 'safe sex' in the shadow of AIDS, with little moral framework for young people to consider.

Children are reaching adolescence two years earlier than children being born 100 years ago. In a recent survey by Bristol University, one in six girls were found to be beginning puberty at the age of eight. The same study of 14,000 children found that one in fourteen boys were entering puberty at the age of eight. This is one of the reasons why children begin to explore sexual relationships earlier. Their bodies if not their emotions are ready younger.

How can we respond to this?

The first big step is to talk about the issues with our children. Sex and abortion are issues more commonly dealt with by youth groups than in Sunday school classes! While it may not be appropriate to go into graphic detail with our primary children, there is much we can do to begin to help them to know what pressure their peers will place on them before it happens. It must be up to parents how much their children are taught about details.

Churches also have a responsibility to train and update their parents, so that they are in a better position to talk with their children.

At home we decided to borrow an American idea with our children at the age of twelve (I suggest younger may have been better). As father in the house I asked my daughter to choose a silver ring, which she wears as a promise ring. From my side, I promise to care, provide and protect her until she leaves home to live on her own or to marry. From her side, she promises to be subject to my headship at home, and not to enter into a sexual relationship until she marries. This is not something my wife or I have imposed. We talked about it, and have entered into a mutual agreement. We all know that we have made promises that may be difficult to keep in the future, and have acknowledged this, but with God's help we are trying to set a good course while she is still young. Prevention is better than cure. If one day my daughter marries, she may choose to replace my silver ring with that given to her by her husband, whose promises will supersede mine.

We have operated with a simple principle in our home. If a child is old enough to ask, they are old enough for a truthful answer. We applied this principle from 'Is Father Christmas real?' to 'Where do babies come from?' To answer the latter question we have found two good books on the facts of life. The first is *Where Do Babies Come From?* published by

Invader. While this is not written from a directly Christian viewpoint, it is clear yet sensitively illustrated. The other book with an overtly Christian perspective is *Who Made Me?* by Malcolm and Meryl Doney, and illustrated by Nick Butterworth and Mick Inkpen. Our children have loved these books from the age of three. Sorry if you were one of those visitors who were introduced to one of them by a friendly five-year-old at story time! At least we know that their introduction to sex education was in our home, and was learned in a Christian context, not initially in the playground.

Drugs and alcohol

- 60 per cent of children are offered recreational drugs by the time they are sixteen years old.

- 60 per cent of children drink alcohol illegally by the time they are sixteen years old.

The availability of drugs to children has grown alarmingly over the last few years, with primary schools finding that children are getting involved younger than ever before. The police are doing more to educate parents and children in primary school, but the church still sees it as a problem for secondary pupils and above.

'Alco-Pops' have made drinking more palatable for children, and brightly coloured labelling, if not designed with children in mind, is certainly very appealing to them.

Television and the Internet

- The average child watches four and a half hours of television every day. The same child spends less than five minutes in direct communication with their father each day.

- More than 50 per cent of children under twelve years old claim to regularly watch videos with a 12 rating or higher.

- More than 50 per cent of children have access to the Internet at home.

It is easy to be judgemental about TV and the communications revolution that is exploding all around us through the Internet, but the new world that is opening up can be educational, exciting and entertaining. Within a very short time children will have to be using the new technology if they are going to get anywhere in life.

The key to setting a godly foundation is talking with our children (not at them!). We need to know what is happening, and where the dangers are, and we need to empower our children to recognise what is unsuitable to watch and help them to decide when to switch off, when to switch over, and when to swap for a video.

One Saturday morning I somewhat grumpily sacrificed my lie-in to sit up and watch Saturday morning TV with my youngest daughter who is usually first up. We were watching a typical Saturday morning children's magazine programme. I was pleased when she said, 'Oh, this cartoon's unsuitable' and turned over to the other side. I didn't even get a chance to make a judgement of my own. Perhaps she was trying to protect my own delicate eyes from *Skeleton Warriors*, but I'm glad she is becoming able to begin to discern for herself. Discernment cannot happen without values, and these need to be adopted by, rather than imposed onto our children before they can begin to select the suitable from the unsuitable.

Values are adopted in a climate of discussion and discovery, where children can work out for themselves what is helpful to watch, and what is unhelpful. The foundation for this is a growing relationship with Jesus, and with Jesus-loving parents.

Videos are great because they provide wider choice and an alternative when that unsuitable programme is on. There are some excellent Christian children's videos around now, that will compete favourably for the affection of any child.

There are an increasing number of excellent Christian family websites to visit. These are not only entertaining, but also provide reviews on films, books, television shows and the latest craze. Parents and children can use these to keep up to date on the good, the bad and the ugly. Try Focus on the Family's website at www.family.org or Children Worldwide at www.childrenworldwide.co.uk.

Some concern must be expressed at the length of time children spend watching TV, however. On average around thirty hours a week. With parents having less one-to-one time with their children, values, attitudes and behaviour patterns are clearly very strongly influenced by television. To break the cycle means a greater effort on the part of parents to spend time with their children and to facilitate their children to be more creative.

One of the effects of watching too much television is that children find it more difficult to use their imaginations when they do play. Children often choose toys that are television characters. They role play what they have seen on television rather than being creative and developing characters from their own imagination. It struck me in Latvia how easily the children played with so little. The same is true in Africa. Children make something out of nothing – an old soft drinks can, some wire and some elastic bands become a racing car. Bracken leaves bound together quickly become a very effective umbrella, and you never seem to hear children say 'I'm bored, I don't know what to do.'

Employment and lifestyle

- Only 16 per cent of children live in a family where the father works and the mother is at home.
- Children in the UK start school younger, and have longer terms, than almost every other country in the world.

The first statistic would be a little higher if you added in families where the mother works and the father is at home, but it would still be less than 20 per cent. This means that most children live in a family where the only parent or both parents are working. Increasingly children are being put into child-care schemes, which can start well before school in the mornings, and finish in the early evening. Parents in full-time employment have little time to spend with their children when they have to keep house as well. For most parents in this situation, there is no choice. It is the only way to make ends meet, but there is an effect on children. On the positive side children develop social skills through spending time with other children and adults. Play schemes can be very creative, keeping children away from the television, but on the negative side, parents have less influence on their children. There is the potential for a weaker relationship, especially if the child is out of parental care much of the time before they start school. Potentially, in these situations, children adopt the values and attitudes of their carers instead of their parents.

Abuse

- 10 per cent of all children experience physical or sexual abuse by the time they are sixteen.
- More than 90 per cent of all abuse takes place in the home.
- Most abusers are friends or family to the children they abuse.

I sometimes sit at the front of a school assembly hall looking out over a sea of faces, and think about the truth of this awful statistic. Uniform smiles, but each face represents a life, and so many of them suffer at the hands of adults The Good Shepherd knows each situation.

Home is the very place where we should feel safe and secure. If children cannot feel safe at home, where do they have to go where they can feel safe?

Most abused children live with it secretly, feeling threatened by the abuser should they disclose what has happened. Many carry the weight of it into middle age or beyond before telling anyone.

CCPAS report that every week parents contact their help line following disclosure that their child has been abused. These reports nearly all come from people who are part of a church. This gives us a glimpse of the size of the problem, and therefore the urgency to make sure we have good practice policies established in our children's work. It also highlights the need for churches to know what to do when abuse is disclosed.

Technology

Here I will just make three simple points that are relevant to children.

1. As technology progresses, and children spend more time with the computer, television and latest computerised toy, they spend less time with people. Technology has the general effect of isolating children. Increasingly people will work from home using computers to communicate, and telephones for conference calls, but spending their coffee break alone. Children spend more time communicating with each other in chat rooms or using M.S.N. on the Internet than face to face.

2. Technology has moved to a point where if something in the house or on the car develops a fault, you throw it away and buy a new 'perfect' one. We placate our consciences by 'recycling' the materials from what we throw away. People are increasingly being treated in the same way. If you don't come up to scratch you will be dumped and replaced. The efficiency of the company is more important than its employees. Instead of the business being there for the sake of the people, the people are there for the sake of the business.

Children are growing up in a 'throw away' age where nothing is worth mending and you have to perform at 100 per cent. The Samaritans published a report recently identifying the main reason for children attempting suicide as being failure to succeed. This tendency for children to be valued on the basis of how good they are at Maths or English puts more pressure on children than ever before, and leaves many feeling inadequate and worthless.

3. In the UK children are used to learning and being entertained with fast-moving, highly visual programmes, whether in the classroom, or on television. While this keeps life exciting, children do not learn to concentrate on one thing for a long time. This has an effect on the way we plan programmes for children. There is a noticeable difference when working with children in a different culture. I remember a trainer solemnly teaching her class of children's workers in Nairobi, 'Children will get bored if they have to sit through a five-hour service.' In England they would not just get bored, they would go out of their minds! We have difficulty engaging children in a Sunday service for more than half an hour. In Africa there is no need to bribe children with points, sweets or prizes to get them to listen to a story or application.

Good practice and political correctness

The enemy is very subtle in the way he goes about his work, especially in the so-called 'developed world'. When we lived in Africa, spiritual forces were far more obvious. Witchdoctors had real power, and most people had seen them at work. We knew one such witch doctor who called down lightning on someone's house as a curse. Very impressive! You will find it very difficult to locate anyone in Central Africa who does not believe in the supernatural. It is such an obvious part of people's lives. Perhaps this acceptance of a spiritual dimension is why there is revival in many parts of Africa, while the church in the UK is dwindling. People there do not find it hard to believe there is a God.

There is one way that the enemy works among our children, which often saddens me. Here I know I am treading on shaky ground, so please read carefully, and don't misunderstand me. The Children Act and the increasing need to be seen to engage in good practice in our work is creating a barrier between workers and children. I am not for one moment suggesting that good practice is a bad thing, or that we should slacken our standards. On the contrary, the church needs to be at the forefront of good practice. Over the last ten years we have worked very hard in our own programmes to improve safety and security wherever possible. There is a challenge though, that we need to overcome if we are to introduce children to Jesus.

I am very moved by this story which comes from a wonderful account of the Sunderland Refreshing by Lois Gott. The book is called *The Glory of His Presence*:

> 'Missus, have you got a hanky?' Lesley, head buried in her thick winter coat, stopped abruptly. Peering around in the gloom, eyes stung by the biting wind, she wondered where the cry had come from.
>
> Searching around in the gloom as faded derelict buildings loomed into view, Lesley thought she must have been mistaken. However, more urgently this time she heard the cry, 'Missus, have you got a hanky?' Cautiously she began to make her way up a darkened alleyway stepping gingerly over debris, bricks and stones. This was a place of utter squalor, reeking of decay. A small figure crouched in the corner, unsuccessfully trying to keep out the cold. His nose streamed and his knees bled. Moving closer, Lesley could see that he was no more than eight years old. Overcome with compassion she

knelt there in the filth to gently wipe the runny nose and attend to his bleeding limbs.

'Why aren't you in school?' she asked.

'I've been bad (north-eastern slang meaning ill or sick) and me mam's kept us off school, but she's gone out and told us not to go back till five o'clock.'

Lesley glanced down at her watch, which read 9.30am, seven and a half hours to wait. Gently cleaning him up she urged him to stay where he was so that she could have someone attend to him immediately. Wiping a tear from her eye she turned to run to the office and a telephone.

'Missus, missus!' She heard the piercing cry again and turned once more to face him. 'Missus, can you give us a kiss?' he asked. Eyes overflowing with tears, Lesley stumbled back up the alley and, bending over the crouched figure, kissed his cold little cheek.'

How many other children are crying out for a hug or a kiss? One of the things we lost with Princess Diana was an out-spoken voice in favour of the hug.

Good practice often means 'don't touch'. How I longed to give Luke a big hug when he told me how his mum had for-gotten to visit him, but in that situation, I knew that it would be inappropriate.

The enemy loves the barrier he has built, which can leave children feeling starved of affection. The challenge for us is to demonstrate the intimate love of Jesus to a lost generation without stepping out of the bounds of good practice.

Let's step back into the Gospels again and look at the example of Jesus.

> *People were bringing little children to Jesus to have him touch them, but the disciples rebuked them. When Jesus saw this, he was indignant. He said to them, 'Let the little children come to me and do not hinder them, for the king-dom of God belongs to such as these. I tell you the truth,*

> *anyone who will not receive the kingdom of God like a little child will never enter it.' And he took the children in his arms, put his hands on them and blessed them.* (Mark 10:13)

The remarkable thing about this incident is that it took place so soon after the sermon we looked at in the first chapter. Both in Matthew and Mark, this incident is recorded in the chapter following Jesus' reply to the disciples asking, *'Who is the greatest in the kingdom of heaven?'* Apparently Jesus' words about the value of children had gone in one ear and straight out the other. No wonder Jesus was indignant, the disciples were treating the children exactly as he had told them not to only a few days earlier. The idea of actually putting Jesus' words into practice was too radical for them. How easy it is to listen to God on Sunday, and then go back to doing what we were doing before on Monday, especially when it relates to children!

Returning to our previous point. Jesus' actions might be seen as close to the line in terms of good practice, if this little incident happened today. His saving grace would be that he only touched the children in the presence of their parents. Here are four phrases from this passage:

– He *touched them.*
– He *took the children in his arms.*
– He *put his hands on them.*
– He *blessed them.*

There is a place for physical touch in communicating the intimate love of the Good Shepherd to children, as long as we work within clear guidelines when we are working with children to whom we are not parents:

1. Always make sure you are not on your own with a child or a group of children. It is particularly important not to touch a child if you are on your own.

2. Respect the relationship you have with the child's family. If you do not know the child's family at all, you may need to avoid physical contact completely, so that no misunderstanding or misrepresentation can occur.

3. Sometimes it is more appropriate for a woman to give physical attention to a child. Sadly, most sexual and physical abuse comes from men. There are occasions when the loving touch of a man is what is needed though.

4. Respect a child's age. It may be appropriate to pick a five-year-old up and give them a hug when they fall over and graze their knee, but this would be less appropriate for a twelve-year-old, where to sit beside them for a few minutes may be better.

5. Respect a child's space. Don't ever touch a child to meet your own needs, only do it to meet theirs. They will seek the touch they need, whether it is a hug after a minor accident, an arm around the child going through family trauma, a lap for the three-year-old who is having a story, or a hand on a walk.

Touch is a very powerful thing. It can convey friendship, love, comfort, guidance, affirmation, sympathy and understanding. No wonder the enemy has devised a society where touch has been all but ruled bad practice.

When we are praying for children it can help just to put a hand on their shoulder. This is not just when we want to impart some blessing. It is a way of identifying with the child as we pray.

In Matthew's version of this incident he finishes with this little phrase: *'When he had placed his hands on them, he went on from there'* (Matthew 19:15).

Matthew makes a point of recording that Jesus went to that particular place with only one thing on his agenda – to bless the children. The disciples had a different agenda. They no doubt thought that there was going to be another healing clinic, or a meeting. Their attempts to get ready for what they thought Jesus was going to do were wasted. The groups of adults sitting hopefully on the ground waiting for another story, the carefully marked out stretcher area, the queue of Pharisees with cunningly worked out trick questions – all would have to wait for another time. When Jesus had finished blessing the children he left!

There are ways of showing Jesus' love to children, other than through touch, but let us not allow the enemy to steal something that is still precious to Jesus, and to the children he loves.

Children, the church and Jesus

- There are twelve million children in the UK.
- 3 per cent or 360,000 regularly attend a church or church group.
- 1000 children are choosing to leave the church every week.

Though new children are joining the church, the massive drain of 1000 every week means that on balance fewer children are attending church every week. The greatest challenge we face in children's ministry today is not how to reach new children, but how to keep the ones we have got.

If things are going to change, we cannot carry on as we are. Something radical needs to happen in our approach to children's ministry. Something radical has to happen to the church, if children are going to be a part of it throughout this century.

The fact is that many people who do not attend a church are heartily sick of what they perceive the church to be. Some of them used to attend church, but have become disillusioned. I don't know too many people who are heartily sick of Jesus. In the past our strategy in children's ministry has been to try and get children to be a part of the church, rather than introduce them to a radical relationship with Jesus. Our emphasis has been on how to get more children (and families) into the church, thereby making the church bigger, rather than seeing an increase in the kingdom of God in our locality. We will look at this in more detail later on.

Summary

Children today are growing up in a disjointed and rapidly changing society, often starved of the basic things they need. They are deeply immersed in a selfish and materialistic culture without absolute moral values. Most are drifting away from God.

Chapter 3

Looking for Lost Sheep

Coming Soon:

Golden Fleece Holiday Club

For all Lost Lambs

At the Fold

Registration from 10am

Starts Monday

Here is a notice that did not go up on the entrance to the sheepfold the day after sheep number one hundred wandered off. The Good Shepherd knew that if he was going to find that lost sheep, he was going to have to:

1. *Leave the ninety-nine on the hills.*
2. *Go to look for the one that wandered off.*

Could there be a lesson here for us?

The fact is that in the UK, ninety-seven sheep are lost for every three that are in the fold. It makes logical sense therefore that if we are going to reach lost children for Jesus, our church building may not be the best place to start.

When Jesus issued the Great Commission to his followers he said 'Go and make disciples.' The emphasis was on going, just as it was for the Good Shepherd. In Acts, Luke records this incident slightly differently:

> *'But you will receive power when the Holy Spirit comes on you; and you will be my witnesses in Jerusalem, and in all Judea and Samaria, and to the ends of the earth.'*
> (Acts 1:8)

Jesus wanted his followers to have a ripple effect. The first impact was to be in their own locality, and then they were to spread out further afield until the whole earth had heard the Good News.

Today, reaching children in the UK needs to be about outreach in the true sense of the word. It calls for missionaries who will leave the security of their building and go to where the lost sheep are. To find them, love them, and begin to relate to them on their territory, not ours. This was the way Jesus did it. The Pharisees hated him for it, accusing him of mixing with tax collectors and sinners, but Jesus pointed out that he had come to seek and to save those who were lost. Sometimes we are more interested in 'saving' than we are 'seeking'.

What does this mean, in the context of reaching children? Where do we need to go to find them, and when we have found them, what should we do with them?

There are three places where you are guaranteed to find children:

1. Home

Unlike some other countries where tens of thousands of children live on the streets, more than 99 per cent of all children in the UK live in a home of some sort.

As the figures in the last chapter suggested, home may not be a happy place for some children, but for most it is a place of security, a hub from which the different aspects of their lives radiate. It is where they will experience the most influential relationships in their lives, where they will sleep and eat and play. It is where they have most free time. It is where some children suffer abuse.

Reaching children at home has its drawbacks. You can only give time to a very few people at once, and so it is very time consuming. A climate of fear means that many doors do not open readily to strangers. Being on someone else's territory will limit what you can say or do, especially to start with.

As part of a strategy for outreach, visiting homes can be enormously fruitful, and very rewarding. We will look at this in more detail as we begin to put together a plan for outreach.

2. School

Chatting with an American teacher friend, we began to compare opportunities for reaching children with the Good News. He teaches in a Christian High School, and is free to share his testimony, talk about Jesus as a personal friend and to pray with his class. How different it is in state schools where there is no Religious Education, and teachers are not allowed to pray, read the Bible or talk about Jesus. Condoms are handed out to students, but the Bible is banned.

In the UK the situation is completely different. Religious Education includes all the major faiths, but at least Christianity is on the curriculum. The law decrees that there should be a 'daily act of worship', and that it should be 'of a broadly Christian nature'. While these two phrases are open to a wide number of interpretations, nobody can argue that there is not an open door into schools for appropriate Christian input. The question is: How long will the door be open? There is increasing pressure from within schools and from interested parties outside schools to change the law and close the door. Much is being done to make the most of the opportunity, but many schools have been abandoned by the church, or the input they receive is seen by the children to be irrelevant and boring. There may come a day when the law is changed and we will be left to rue a great, lost opportunity.

When it comes to finding children, school is another good starting place.

3. Play

This covers the recreational world of children from the theme park to the street corner. Anywhere that children go to have fun and spend time with their friends. Since friendship is one of the vital keys to child evangelism, and since all children need some form of recreation, this too is a good place to start.

Scripture Union and CSSM have known about this for generations, running beach missions around the coasts of the British Isles where many hundreds of children have begun a relationship with Jesus.

Responding to what I felt was a growing call to serve God among children, as a teenager I got to know the coast of North Wales pretty well. Children's workers were disguised in fancy dress in the park at Colwyn Bay, so that children could find us and use the secret pass phrase – 'Did you have kippers for breakfast?' or 'Is that your nose you're wearing?' I remember that several children asked the latter question to a little Jewish gentleman who was sitting minding his own business on a bench! Sadly the days of 'Hunt the Leader' have all but passed with increased fears about the safety of children asking strange people weird questions in the park! I got to know the little village of Nefyn very well, especially the steep hill running down to the beach, which seemed to grow as the summer progressed. One little Bible group I had was made up of children who could only speak Welsh. Why I was asked to take this group I don't know. I confess that my only Welsh word (of which I am very proud) is Llanfairpwllgwyngyllgogerillwryndrabollantysiliogogo. Unfortunately this word is very limited as a tool for evangelism, as it is the name of a small village on the island of Anglesea. Armed with the grace of God and a Welsh New Testament, which I still have, we somehow managed to make friends, and one small boy gave his life to Jesus. This proves that God's Welsh is better than mine, and the story could end happily there, but it didn't. Young Ewan decided he wanted to write to me. He wrote in Welsh, and I lived in Little-hampton, Sussex (before Delirious!). To my surprise I found that there was a lady at Littlehampton library who could not only speak Welsh but also read it, so she interpreted Ewan's letters, and the replies, which had to be changed into Welsh. What a wonderful witness to this kind lady as she heard about Ewan's new faith!

Anyway, enough of reminiscing! I hope we have established that where children go to play, there is an opportunity to show them the love of Jesus.

Having established that there are three places to find lost children (other than Bournemouth beach), let's begin to put the whole thing into shape.

What about a strategy?

Children's work is often undertaken in a rather ad hoc way.

Imagine if you will, for a moment, a game of rugby. An expectant buzz rises excitedly around the ground. The ref blows the whistle and the opposition kicks off. As they do so the pack get together on one side of the pitch for a team talk. The fullback fetches another ball and begins to practise his goal kicks, and the forwards practise a line out. The opposition has no difficulty in running the ball through for their first try.

There are two problems to this approach. First, the team has obviously not grasped the fact that when the whistle blows you stop practising and start to play. Secondly, there is no sense of team. Everyone is doing his own thing.

Sometimes church-based children's ministry can be like this. A variety of excellent activities takes place, but no one has ever sat down to ask the questions 'What is our strategy?' 'What are our goals?' and 'Will the activities we have planned help us to reach our objectives?' Be careful. The answers to these questions could radically change your kids' work!

There are three main objectives in Children's ministry:

1. To serve children in the community or in areas of need, in Jesus' name, for the sake of doing good. Establishing God's values in society. In this way we are involved in the business of seeing God's kingdom established in our area. This is something that Jesus taught his disciples to pray for.

2. Outreach, with the goal of finding lost lambs, and helping them to come into a saving knowledge of Jesus. Evangelism.

3. Training children to become dynamic followers of Jesus. Discipleship.

Arguably none of these objectives stands on its own, but there may be seasons in your ministry, or in the life of your church, when it will be right to emphasise one over the other. Since we all have different gifts and callings, it may be that you are called to one of these areas and not all three. The key thing is that we identify what we are trying to achieve.

So how do we go about it?

In this chapter we are looking at outreach and evangelism. To help assess what your church is doing, and to plan a strategy for the future, it may be helpful to draw a flow chart or a 'stepping stone' chart. The main emphasis for the children's work in our local church at the moment is on discipleship, rather than evangelism, though interestingly we have seen a number of new children coming into the group and getting saved recently. Before that we had a season of prioritising outreach. We used a stepping stone strategy, which looked something like this:

	Home	School	Play	Church
Step 1	Visit all homes to talk about our children's activities	Assemblies	Summer fun days	
Step 2	Visit interested families again	Lessons and special events	Face painting and clowning at fetes, etc.	B-B-Qs and fun events

	Home	School	Play	Church
Step 3	Visiting with invitations for Holiday Club			Holiday Club
Step 4	Weekly visits to homes of children attending	Visits to schools to pray	Outings to Bowling and Skating	Children's clubs for 5-7s and 7-11s
Step 5	Weekly visits to homes of children attending	Lunch-time clubs		All-age meetings
Step 6	Weekly visits to homes of children attending			Nurture Group

As you can see, there are some gaps, and this raises an important practical point. Person power. (Manpower would be great, but as we have already seen, it is mostly girl-power!) You can only set up a strategy based on the number of people you have available to make it happen.

I have marked in the areas that we actually did in plain text, and I have added in a lot more home visitation, which we did not have the manpower for. The reason I have done this is because I believe it would have made our work a lot more effective, in terms of drawing in new children, developing relationships, following up those who drifted away, and drawing in whole families.

In recent years Bill Wilson has made a huge impact in the whole area of outreach to children, not just in the UK, but world-wide. He has developed a ministry in some of the toughest parts of New York that has seen tens of thousands of children coming to faith in Jesus. A number of cities in the UK including Liverpool, Leeds and Sheffield have picked up his model and are adapting it to the British culture. One of the strongest elements of Metro Ministries is commitment to regular visitation to the same homes week after week. Leaders are going to where children are and beginning to build relationships with whole families. Transport is provided to bring children to regular events where they can hear the gospel and begin to follow Jesus.

Drawing up a neat chart and rearranging your children's activities will not be enough to bring revival to the children in your home town. There are some important keys to seeing children coming into a relationship with Jesus.

Calling and commitment

There was nothing glamorous for the Good Shepherd about taking up his crook and lantern and setting off into the gathering dusk to look for his wayward lamb. The only thing that made him do it was a love for the one he had lost. That same love made him persevere until the lamb was found. That same love overwhelmed him with joy as he carried the lost lamb home.

The first key to reaching children is a sense of calling and commitment on behalf of those who will be involved. It is not a glamorous job, and it is still sometimes given a low priority by the church as a whole. Though men may not often honour this ministry, as we have seen the King of Kings thinks very highly of it, and this must be a source of encouragement to those who work with children.

Children's ministry is very tiring. It is physically tiring. Often it is emotionally and spiritually tiring. Children's workers need to be very resourceful, and there is a need for perseverance. Most children's workers serve by running weekly groups that soon lose their novelty. Going out on a cold Thursday evening to run a weekly children's club does not always feel exciting, but God can refresh and re-impassion children's workers.

Church leaders can help by providing regular training and encouragement, and remembering to say thank you to the children's team from time to time.

A serving attitude

Here's another good biblical theme best demonstrated by none other than Jesus himself. Whether we are visiting homes or schools, we are guests on someone else's patch. Our attitude will be conveyed long before we are able to say anything about Jesus, and whether we are welcome or not will depend on how we come across. Since Jesus has said that we should be child-like if we want to enter the kingdom of heaven, let's learn to be like the children we visit without being childish.

In schools this may mean offering to help out on a school fete or sports day, to make cups of tea at a parents' evening, or be on call to help in an emergency. At home it may mean being ready to take the rubbish out on your way, or drop some letters in at the post box. These acts of service say more about the love of Jesus than many words.

In building relationships with children we will need to be honest and transparent. Back to being humble again!

A few weeks ago I was helping to plan and present a children's event which to be quite honest turned out to be downright boring! I had encouraged our children to attend, and painted a very rosy picture of what we hoped the event would be like. The following Thursday I could do nothing other than apologise to the children, for a bad afternoon out!

Then there was the day my dad died. Facing bereavement was a new experience for me. It left me with such a mixture of emotions and sometimes no emotions at all. It was great to be able to talk to the children about what had happened, and for them to pray for me. It is not always easy to be this open, well not for me anyway, but when we are it deepens our friendship with our children and makes it easier for them to be open with us. This week, two of our children have lost their grand-dad. They know that I know how they feel.

Training

'I feel called to serve God as a missionary in Papua New Guinea.' The missionary committee listens attentively to the young man as he pours out his heart, and then they begin to advise him. 'Take a year to get more experience in secular work while serving on the church mission team, then go on a short-term hit squad to see if you are really cut out for it. Apply to Bible School or a vocational training scheme, and build up a network of supporters who can pray for you and provide for some of your needs. Make up a visual display that you can use to share your vision.' Sometimes it seems to take forever to get to where you think God is calling you. With children's workers it is often quite the opposite.

'Please let Mrs Jenkins know if you can help out with teaching Sunday school. The situation is desperate. No experience is called for. This is a particularly suitable post for anyone who is bored with the adult meetings.' You sign up, and after two weeks of watching Mrs Jenkins, you are a Sunday school teacher. You might stay that way for thirty years without ever getting any training or refreshing.

Child evangelism is a very specialist area. It is challenging and demanding. An inappropriate attitude or approach can result in a home or a school remaining closed to Christians for a generation.

Apart from a careful recruitment and referencing system, workers should also be properly trained. This may take time, but will bear fruit in the long run.

Training is available in many different shapes and sizes, from inter-church Saturday training days, to year-long residential courses.

There are two distinct categories of training needed for children's workers:

1. *Start-up Training.* For new recruits. They need to have a basic biblical foundation for working with children, some

basic practical skills like story telling, and how to organise a programme for a particular age group. Finally, it is important that they have a good grounding in essential legal requirements, and that they understand the church's policy for good practice.

2. *Refresher Training.* Many workers have faithfully served God and the church with children for many years. It is common to find workers who are tired and dry. They have never been offered the opportunity to go on something designed to renew their strength and revitalise their vision. When Steph and I came into working full time with children in 1984, we decided, on some wise person's advice, that each year we would look for something that would provide us with training and spiritual refreshment. We have endeavoured to keep our 'L' plates on ever since, and do not intend taking them off until it is time to go to heaven! Over the years we have feasted on a rich diet. Sometimes we have gone on courses specifically for kids' workers with Scripture Union or Kings Kids for example, and sometimes we have been to conferences with the words 'Fire', 'River' or 'Wind' in them hoping to get some of those elements into our bellies! We are thankful to God that we have been able to do these things, which on paper have often looked out of reach financially. On other occasions we have learned new skills on counselling courses or learning to sign. The principle is one we would recommend to anyone. Don't stop learning. Be humble enough to go back to basics, and plan it into your year.

If you have responsibility for a team of children's workers, whether in evangelism or any other area of ministry, one of the best things you can do for your children is to make sure your workers get the training and refreshment they need.

Training does not only have the benefit of equipping team members, it also lets them know that they are valued. An encouraged worker operates much better than a discouraged worker.

A helping hand

Back to our stepping stone strategy.

My primary education took place at Sakeji school, a boarding school in northern Zambia established for the education of missionary children, which my mother had attended as one of the first pupils. To get there for her meant being carried on a hammock complete with umbrella for several days through the bush. For me, with the advent of modern technology, and the odd war, the journey had changed to Land-Rover, motorboat avoiding blown-up bridge, and ancient lorry.

On Sundays the oldest children would set off on a walk of about two miles to get to the church meeting. Being allowed to leave the school grounds was always exciting. Our route took us across a grassy plain dotted with wild iris and orchids, down to some thick forest on the edge of the Sakeji River. Large stepping stones had been placed in the river to create a crossing point. These could only be used in the dry season when the stones emerged from what could be a raging torrent in the wet season. In my memory, distorted no doubt by age, these stones seemed quite far apart, and in the middle of the river there was a point where the gap between stones was noticeably bigger than all the other gaps. The water here seemed to run faster and deeper. An adult would always stand over this gap to give a helping hand to those crossing, and there was always a sense of relief and excitement when you were over.

One of the advantages of looking at our outreach model in terms of stepping stones is that we can look at the gaps to see if they are too big, and ask ourselves how we are going to help children get across. The gap for most children between school assembly and being an integrated member of your local church is far too big. Don't be surprised if you advertise a wonderful all-age meeting next time you do an assembly to find that none of the children come! There needs to be a number of other levels at which children can engage. If instead you advertise a fun day in your local park, or even a barbecue in the church car park, you are much more likely to have some success.

You may go armed with good publicity but the chances are, your beautiful computerised invitation will still be ignored, treated sceptically, and probably made into a paper plane, which you will see lying on the road next time you go shopping.

Having stepping stones with small gaps in between is a move in the right direction but, just as with the river crossing, children will still need a helping hand to get across. The helping hand can only come from someone they know, like and trust. This is where visiting at home can begin to make a difference. If the child gets the invitation at school *and* someone they have got to know calls and offers to take them, then there is a much bigger chance they will come, and so the process of helping children take steps towards Jesus begins.

A helping hand can come from a leader who has invested time in building a relationship with the child and their family.

An even more effective helping hand can come from those children who are already following Jesus, and have been trained to reach out to their friends.

Imagine the child in school who has heard you enthuse about your planned fun day in the park. If a Christian friend in his class says: 'I'm going to the fun day on Saturday, would you like to come with me?' the chances of success are even higher. This raises the whole area of training our Christian kids to be effective disciples. We will be looking at this in some detail later on.

Non-religious, relevant, and exciting programmes

Don't try to say that with a mouthful of coffee!

Now we have a nice stepping stone strategy grid. We have leaders with a sense of calling, who are being trained to serve. We are beginning to build relationships with children and their families, but there is still a problem! The fun day was great, but our midweek club is boring, and the three children who came to a Sunday meeting left halfway through and promised never to come back! What's wrong?

Reaching children is far more effectively done in their world than it is in ours.

We have already seen that if we want to find lost sheep we need to go to where children are, but we must return to another principle we have started to look at. Our aim is primarily to introduce children to Jesus, not to make them a part of our church. It is true that children need to belong to the church, but belonging to a boring church without really knowing Jesus is the worst of both worlds!

In accessing our programme we need to look at what the children in our locality like doing. Where do they spend their time, and on what do they spend their money!?

A member of our church did just such a survey recently. We found that the sports centre was the most popular place for children in our town, with swimming coming up as number one activity. Football, uniformed groups, after-school clubs and a whole diversity of other activities followed. If we are going to plan a programme that will appeal to children we need to understand what they like doing, and plan those things in. It is also worth looking at activities that are not available in your immediate locality and organising outings slightly further afield. If given the choice, the children in our midweek group always choose ice skating, ten pin bowling or a sleepover as their first choices. The first two are not available in Dronfield, but can be found within half an hour.

There is no escape for weary leaders from the annual sleepover that has become a big favourite with the children. Sleep does get sacrificed it is true, but it does provide a great opportunity for spending focussed time with the children, and for some of them, it is their first experience of sleeping away from home and parents. Obviously the sleepover needs to be properly organised and staffed, and a cooked breakfast will be a great way to finish.

Exciting does not necessarily have to mean high-tech. In fact, children may well find it more exciting, in an age when they watch four hours of TV every day, to go for an adventure walk rather than play another video game.

Jesus was often seen to stand against the religion of his day. He hated the way the Pharisees put the law above compassion. In his day religion had actually become a barrier between ordinary people and God, particularly if they were classified as 'sinners'. Religion was all about trying to keep a set of rules, many of which had been made up by the religious leaders rather than taken from the Torah. The Pharisees believed that it was only possible to please God by keeping all the correct regulations, and they acted as judge and jury for anyone who didn't. Jesus respected the Torah, never speaking against it, but his lifestyle showed that he had no time for 'religion' if it kept people away from God.

A close look at ourselves will show that whatever flavour church we belong to, acceptable practices and good ways of doing things can easily turn into inflexible regulations and unhelpful traditions. Even the language we use quickly becomes jargon if we are not careful. Jesus did not use jargon. Ordinary people loved him because they did not feel alienated from him. They could plainly understand him. He did not have the disadvantage of trying to get people to come into a weird building that 'smells of dead people', to quote my youngest daughter.

Religion is still one of the biggest blocks to children coming into a relationship with Jesus.

Growing up as a child in a missionary family meant I often got the chance to listen to some choice phrases. What do these phrases mean to a child?

'Lord we thank you for taking Mrs Jones to be with you this week, and now we pray that you will undertake for her husband.'

'On Thursday night we will be opening up Peter in the back room.'

'Next week's speaker is pinned in the vestibule.'

'Please leave your hymnbook at the door as you pass out.'

'Now let us pray for those who are sick of this assembly.'

'We pray for Mr Jones who is laid aside upon a bed of sickness.' (Yuk!)

'Now may we have the intimations?'

Ah! I hear you cry. This language is old-fashioned. We don't speak like that in our church. Modern churches have their jargon too! When we first joined a 'new church' we had been praying for new office premises. Someone came to us and said, 'I have a picture of you in the Peel Centre.' I ignorantly protested that I had never been in the Peel Centre, so I considered this to be impossible. 'No,' they protested 'not a photo, a picture.' I continued to look blank. Slowly and concisely they began to explain that the picture had been given to them by God, and I began to realise that they were talking about a picture in their minds, not something physical! We can even use good, sound biblical language as jargon. Excellent words like salvation, righteousness, redemption and grace are nothing more than jargon until they are explained. When we use them they become a barrier if they are understood by the user but not the listener.

What does this conjure up for a child?:

'The ministry team will be waiting for you at the front.'

'Let's take time to soak in the river this morning.'

'She's an anointed speaker.'

'On Tuesday there will be a waiting on the Lord meeting.'

'The Jones' cell will be meeting at the Browns' this week.'

If we are to be relevant to the children we are seeking to reach we need to have a reasonable knowledge of the things that are held to be important to them. We need to know which pop groups are selling the most CDs, which football team gets the most support, and how they are doing. What is the latest craze? We need to know what is happening in the soaps they watch and what their favourite cartoons are. This does not mean that we need to spend our whole lives immersed in these things, but we need to have a working knowledge of them. If you are not sure what is going on, ask your children, they'll tell you. When you are speaking, pick up illustrations from their world. There is a rich source of illustration on video.

Chapter 4

Going Fishing

Throwing out the net

Sorry about the change of metaphor. Up till now we have been looking for lost sheep, now we are going fishing.

Peter knew about fishing. He was a fisherman. When Jesus wanted to call Peter he went into his world, not just physically – giving the tip of the day for where to drop that net – but also verbally, using Peter's language. *'Come, follow me,' Jesus said, 'and I will make you fishers of men'* (Mark 1:17).

Fishing is a good metaphor for evangelism because there are two important stages to fishing with a net – 1. Throwing it out; and 2. Pulling it in. If you prefer to use a rod, the cast comes before reeling the fish in. In many ways the throwing out of the net, or the cast, is more important and demands more skill and experience than the pulling in. Peter knew every eddy and crag on that lake. He knew just how to cast the net so that it would cover the greatest possible area without causing disturbance to the fish. Any amount of pulling in the net was useless if the net had not been thrown out in the right place.

To reach children for Jesus there needs to be a throwing out of the net. Entering into their world, and earning the right to talk to them through building a relationship with them, will do part of this. The other part will be done through planning a programme that includes teaching as well as evangelism.

Children cannot respond to a Jesus whom they know nothing about. A foundation of understanding needs to be laid before the net can be pulled in. So what is the minimum that a child needs to understand so that they can come into a saving relationship with Jesus?

Let me introduce you to Jake. He is ten years old. He lives at home with his mum, and likes riding his bike, and playing football on the green. He is a regular guy. On Sundays he goes to see his dad or his grandparents. Sometimes he gets into trouble at school for fighting. His best friend is Mike. Jake has heard the word Jesus before. His mum uses it as a swear word sometimes, but if he uses it he gets a clip around the ear. At school the vicar uses the word sometimes when he prays. He doesn't get a clip round the ear from anyone! Very confusing.

Jake's friend, Mike, goes to your church, and he has asked Jake to go to the summer holiday club called Gladiators. During the week, Jake has found out that Jesus is a human being, and has heard some exciting stories about him. This will be a stepping stone towards Jesus for Jake, but it might take months or even years before Jesus becomes a personal Saviour to him. On the other hand, he might choose to follow Jesus this week. What is the minimum he needs to know before he can do that?

Here are some of the most important foundation stones.

Who is God?

God exists. God is all-powerful. He planned the world and everyone in it. He made the world and keeps it going. He loves people of all sorts. He loves bad people as well as good. He wants to be our heavenly Father.

Who is Jesus?

Jesus is God's Son, making him a part of God as well as human. He has always existed. He is alive and living in heaven now. He will live for ever. He is perfect, having never done anything wrong. Jesus wants to have a relationship with us.

Who am I?

I am planned and created by God. I was made in his image. He loves me, and wants me to be adopted into his family.

What is sin?

Sin is anything I think, say or do that does not please God. God and Jesus have never sinned. They hate sin, but still love sinners. Every other person in the world has sinned. Sin separates us from God. We cannot become part of God's family until our sin has been dealt with. The punishment for sin is death.

What has God done about this?

God has chosen his Son Jesus to be punished for all the sins of the world. He died on the cross to take the punishment we deserve, and came back to life to prove that death can be defeated. Now anyone who chooses, can receive God's forgiveness if they turn away from their sin. God offers everlasting life to anyone who is adopted into his family.

What must I do about this?

God's forgiveness is only effective when we – 1. Humble ourselves to repent; 2. Ask for it. When we do this sincerely God will always adopt us into his family, and no one can snatch us away from him.

Then what?

Becoming part of God's family is not something that happens just for a week at a holiday club. Part of repenting and asking

Jesus to forgive us, is counting the cost of following Jesus in the future. We need to think about the implications for following Jesus at home and at school, and we need to think about how we can continue to meet with God's people.

When we receive God's forgiveness he does not leave us struggling to live for him by ourselves. Part of being adopted means that God's Holy Spirit comes to live in us. He can empower us to live as sons and daughters of our heavenly Father.

If I were a theologian, I would probably end up writing a book instead of a page on the question of what Jake needs to know, but I am not, and Jesus said: *'I tell you the truth, unless you change and become like little children, you will never enter the kingdom of heaven'* (Matthew 18:3). Sometimes we want to complicate the core of the gospel, thinking that this gives it more weight, when actually all it does is make it less accessible to the ordinary person that Jesus loves.

This does not mean that there is not an unfathomable depth to understanding God or the mysteries of his word. We have a lifetime after we are adopted into God's family to begin to get to grips with God, and we have eternity for the process to continue. But to receive Jesus as my Saviour is gloriously simple to understand. Simple enough, surprise, surprise, for a child to understand.

The headings I have used might be arranged into the daily subjects for a seven-day holiday club. Over the years we have used many themes for our holiday clubs, from Gladiators to the Wild West, Thunderback 7 Time Machine to the Garden Party. Each time we have woven these essential truths together to provide a foundation for children who are hearing the gospel for the first time, and to try to clarify it for those for whom the jigsaw puzzle is incomplete.

You may have noticed that having started talking about

lost sheep, and having swapped to the idea of fishing, we have now changed the metaphor once more!

Jesus used lots of different pictures to help his audiences to understand the idea of being lost and needing to be found. Many more than three. So I feel justified in making the change too. Each time Jesus used a different picture, it was so that he could emphasise a different point. I have chosen to use the idea of being adopted into God's family in the outline above for a good reason. I think Jake might get a bit confused if I describe him as a lost sheep, or an un-caught fish. When I am talking to him I want to use language that will make sense to him.

What would Jake understand from these ideas?

1. The lost sheep

This is a story about physically being found and rescued. Jake does not like being compared with an animal that is renowned for being dumb. What is this fold he is being brought back into anyway? The sheep does not need to do anything to get rescued. It just waits for the Good Shepherd to turn up.

2. The fish

The fish is definitely a lot better off before he is caught and thrown flapping into the bottom of a smelly boat. A bit tricky to explain this one.

3. Inviting Jesus into your heart?

This is the idea I grew up with, and it is still widely used today.

Young children think literally. Jake is beginning to be able to understand metaphors, but sometimes he still struggles to separate what people mean literally and what they mean metaphorically. At holiday club some of the children are five years old. For them the idea of asking Jesus into your heart is pretty gruesome! Your heart is not very big, and it has loads of blood pumping through it. For a full-grown man to get in there will mean a messy operation, and what will he do when he gets there? Who wants to ask Jesus to come into their heart? No? Oh well, let's try something else.

4. Having Jesus as your best friend

This is a bit better. No messy operation and Jake understands the idea of having a best friend. So do the younger children on the front row of your holiday club.

The trouble is that Jake has a different best friend this week from the one he had last week, and if his best friend doesn't share his crisps with him on Monday, he might fall out with him, and find someone else to play with. There is no agreement or cost involved in becoming someone's best friend, it just kind of happens!

This idea is a bit weak.

5. Having Jesus as your Saviour

Surely this one has got to be a winner. It is very biblical.

As we have seen, part of what Jake needs to understand before he can join God's family, is that Jesus has been punished instead of him, and that he needs to be forgiven. Understanding that Jesus is a 'saviour' or 'rescuer' is very important. After all, his name, Jesus, means Saviour. Gabriel told Joseph: *'You are to give him the name Jesus, because he will save his people from their sins'* (Matthew 1:21).

The problem is that Jesus is not *only* a Saviour. If Jake only understands that God can rescue him, he may not understand anything about the ongoing relationship God wants to have with him. The holiday club will become a rescue point in his memory, but he may have trouble becoming a disciple.

6. Becoming a Christian

This is also a good biblical idea. The nickname Christian was first used for Jesus' disciples in Antioch in the first century, and Peter writes: *'If you suffer as a Christian, do not be ashamed, but praise God that you bear that name'* (1 Peter 4:16).

One of the problems with using this idea, is that different denominations have different teachings on what makes someone a Christian. Many children believe that they become a Christian when they are christened. Jake has never decided to follow Jesus himself but he will probably think he is already a Christian, because he has been christened, He knows nothing about Jesus, and only goes to church for weddings, funerals and some other christenings. Now he's confused.

Becoming a Christian does better convey the idea of living his life for Jesus, but there is no hint of cost or a point of repentance.

7. Joining God's family

This is the idea I prefer to use with children, though I have heard some of the above used very effectively.

First, the idea is one that Jesus used. The story of the lost son is perhaps even more gripping than the story of the lost sheep, because this time it is a human being that has wandered away, so straight away Jake can relate more easily. In the story, one of the keys to being received back into his father's house was a decision on behalf of the lost boy as he sat gazing at the smelly pigs in front of him. He made the decision to repent and return to his father.

God has already done everything necessary for Jake to be rescued, but now a decision has to be made by him.

The story of the lost or prodigal son fits in directly with the way that God has chosen to relate to us. When Jesus taught his disciples to pray he began with *'Our Father'*. When he talked to his disciples about God he used the phrase *'Your Father in heaven'*.

In Paul's letters this idea is further developed. To the Ephesians, he writes: *'In love he predestined us to be adopted as his sons through Jesus Christ'* (Ephesians 1:5). To the Galatians he writes: *'You are all sons of God through faith in Christ Jesus'* (Galatians 3:26). Paul's teaching explains how we become God's children. It is not by birth. We are all born with a sinful nature. We become God's children when he adopts us. This adoption happens when we repent and put our faith in Jesus. John picks up the same theme in his letters, when he writes: *'How great is the love the Father has lavished on us, that we should be called children of God! And that is what we are!'* (1 John 3:1).

In summary, God has made it possible for us to be adopted into his family. This happens when we choose to receive his gift of forgiveness and eternal life. When it happens, God becomes our heavenly Father.

This new family membership is not a formal, religious arrangement; it is an intimate and privileged position. Paul puts it this way: *'You received the Spirit of sonship. And by him we cry "Abba Father"'* (Romans 8:15). The closest translation for 'Abba' is 'Daddy'. It is the cry of a *teknon* or small child towards their loving daddy.

As if this were not enough, we also get a new brother. In Hebrews 2:11 we read: *'Both the one who makes men holy and those who are made holy are of the same family. So Jesus is not ashamed to call them brothers.'*

This means that spiritually our relationship with each other is of the same generation. We are all children of God if we are believers, whether we are three years old or ninety-three. We are all brothers and sisters in Christ whatever our age. We have no right to treat our younger brothers and sisters any differently from anyone else.

Joining God's family is a much stronger metaphor than being best friends. It carries with it a number of important truths:

- Adoption is a binding agreement. It lasts for a lifetime.
- An adopted child is chosen.
- Joining a family means we gain a father, and brothers and sisters.
- As God's children we acknowledge his right as head of the family to direct and discipline us.
- As God's sons (male and female!) we inherit all the riches of our heavenly Father.
- As God's children we will one day live with him in heaven.

The idea of joining God's family can be helpful in explaining how we first come to faith. It also provides a great framework for developing the idea of discipleship.

There is one loud objection to this idea, and this is why many people keep away from the analogy of family. They will say that family has broken down to the extent that many children will not find it helpful. How can we tell children that God wants to be their father, when the only father they have known has been abusive? How can we use this idea when many children have lost contact with their father and don't even know what it is like to have a father about?

I would say this is the very reason why we should teach children that God is a perfect father. Children who have lost touch with their dad need to know that God wants to be a dad to them. He will not take the place of an earthly dad. His relationship with us is different, but he can fill the gap that an absent dad leaves. He is always reliable, he never breaks a promise, and he always wants the best for us. He is always present, and whatever we do, his love for us never changes. It is a beautiful thing to see a fatherless child beginning to develop a father relationship with God. In some ways their relationship is even more meaningful than for a child with two parents living at home.

The parenthood of God is also an encouragement to single mums or dads. I am brought back again to the fact that God is a single parent. He has within him all the attributes of a perfect father. He also has within him all the attributes of a perfect mother. I love this beautiful verse from Deuteronomy 33:27. The words of Moses: *'The eternal God is your refuge, and underneath are the everlasting arms.'* Moses knew what it was to find refuge in the arms of a protective mother. It was she that looked after him secretly and illegally until the day he was placed in the Nile. It was she who continued to look after him when he was taken into the palace by Pharaoh's daughter. The truth of their relationship to each other stayed a closely-guarded secret. Hundreds of years later as Jesus looked out over Jerusalem, he cried: *'How often I have longed to gather your children together, as a hen gathers her chicks under her wings'* (Matthew 23:37). Here is that same maternal love demonstrated in God's Son, Jesus.

Drawing in the net

Joshua was a great leader of God's people. He saw the Israelites in the land God had promised to his ancestors, but he often got frustrated with the attitude of the people, who so quickly drifted away from God. Before his death he called all the people together at Shechem and reminded them of the history of God's faithfulness to them. At the end of his summary he issued a challenge to the people: *'Now fear the Lord and serve him with all faithfulness. Throw away the gods your forefathers worshipped beyond the River and in Egypt, and serve the Lord. But if serving the Lord seems undesirable to you, then choose for yourselves this day whom you will serve'* (Joshua 24:14-15).

The people were brought to a point of decision. Joshua did not ask the people to go away and think about it, he told them to choose today!

Back to fishing.

There is no point in throwing out a fishing net, however skilfully, and then leaving it forgotten. The whole point of throwing it out is so that it can be pulled in at the right time, with fish in it.

Part of the process of outreach is to provide the right opportunity for children to respond to the gospel by accepting God's forgiveness and a place in his family. For this to happen, specific opportunities need to be built into our kids' programme. How do we go about this?

1. Don't bash the children with their need to repent every week! This is like trailing a lobster pot behind a boat in the hope of catching a lobster! Children will become hardened to this approach, like Pharaoh who hardened his heart to Moses.

2. Don't scare your children into the kingdom! My childhood was spent in churches where the doctrine of the Second Coming of Jesus was taught at every possible opportunity, and I was sure the 'Rapture' was going to come before my tenth birthday. A lack of assurance meant I sometimes used to creep into my parents' bedroom to make sure they had not been whisked off to glory leaving me behind. It frightened me! One night I lay on my bed and just asked the Lord to give me an assurance that I would go too. There was no flash of light or angelic manifestation, but I do remember getting a wonderful sense of assurance that has not left me to this day.

   While I do not think that hell should be a taboo subject in children's work, 'dangling children over the pit' could rightly be described as manipulation.

3. Don't paint a rosy picture of what being a part of God's family is like. Jesus reminded his disciples that before anyone builds a tower, he must calculate the cost and, perhaps even more pertinent to children who are disciples, he said that before you go to war, you should check out the opposition.

The truth is that living the life of a committed Christian as a child is extremely tough, and there is a cost to calculate. Our oldest son, Daniel, suffered a lot of bullying in his junior school. His faith was one of the targets for the bullies. On one occasion, as we discussed his problems with his teacher, the teacher said: 'If only he would not talk about his faith, he would not be picked on nearly so much.' Junior school is one of the toughest places to live out a Christian life.

4. Don't compartmentalise your evangelism too much. Valuable opportunities will be lost if evangelism is confined to the annual holiday club. Plan specific evangelistic programmes into your Sunday and midweek programmes. Camps, holidays and weekends away are great for this too.

Thursday evening approaches. You are planning to have a special evangelistic evening for your kids' club. Months of 'net throwing' have preceded this special evening. Jake has been coming to the club quite regularly since the holiday club he attended with his friend. Mike calls for him each Thursday evening so that he has someone to come with. Jake heard all about Jesus at holiday club and how he loves us and died for us on the cross, but it was all new and strange to him. Since then he has been hearing stories from the Old Testament and has learned more about God's greatness and how sin spoils people's lives.

How can you provide the right opportunity for Jake to choose to join God's family?

1. Make sure all your team know what you are planning.

2. Pray.

3. Tell the children early in the programme that there will be a chance to talk and pray with someone if they want to come into God's family.

4. Use a Bible story that the Holy Spirit can help you apply to the children. The Prodigal Son, Zacchaeus, Jesus' death and resurrection. There are many more to choose from.

5. Make space in your programme for children to respond. Fifteen to twenty minutes may be about right. Explain when this time will be.

6. Identify a specific place that children can come to if they want to respond. Make sure this is not out of sight of everyone else. It needs to be open to view, and accessible for parents. Keep it informal.

7. Identify the people who will be there for children to respond to. This will help children not to worry about whom they will talk to. Have at least one male and one female available to chat. Where possible boys should be counselled by boys, and girls by girls.

When the child responds

1. Be a midwife. You can't bring about the process of being born again. Only the Holy Spirit can do that. Your job is to facilitate what God is doing. Just as it is possible for a baby to be born prematurely, so it is possible to try to press a child to make a commitment. This is manipulation. If you think the child is not ready, chat with them, answer their questions, pray with them and let them go.

2. Be on the same level. Sit on chairs or on the floor, but do not tower over the child.

3. Use the child's name. If you don't know what it is, ask them. Write it down so you don't forget.

4. Ask them why they have come, and give them time to answer. Resist the temptation to put words into their mouths. If they are nervous, it may take a little while for them to answer.

5. Just deal with their enquiry, and then ask if there is anything else they want to talk about. If not, let them go. A zealous counsellor I heard of once counselled a child non-stop through to a prayer of commitment, only to find out when he asked a final 'Is there anything else you want to know?' that the child had only come forward because he had lost his coat!

6. Use some children's counselling material. Keep it in stock as an act of faith! There are a number of different ones you can use, from Scripture Union, Children Worldwide, or Ishmael. Have your Bible on hand. The counselling material will include Bible verses, but you might like to look some up in your Bible to show that what you are talking about is rooted in God's word, not just the counselling book.

7. If the child indicates that they want to make some kind of a response to the gospel, introduce them to the material you are going to use, and ask them if they would like to read it with you. Remember that some children can't read, so be careful not to embarrass them.

8. As you go through the material, ask questions that do not have a 'yes/no' answer, to see how much the child understands. This will help you to discern whether they are ready to make a commitment.

9. Counselling books contain a prayer that the child can use to verbalise their response. Rather than saying the prayer for them, encourage the child to read or say the prayer. If they cannot read, offer to say the prayer with them. You can say a few words at a time, and they can echo you.

10. Encourage the child. They may feel emotional about what has happened. They may not feel anything at all. Thankfully our salvation does not depend on how we feel. Use Bible verses to show that God accepts everyone

who comes to him, and that God will keep us safe in his family.

. . . to all who received him, to those who believed in his name, he gave the right to become children of God (John 1:12).

'My sheep listen to my voice; I know them, and they follow me. I give them eternal life, and they shall never perish; no one can snatch them out of my hand' (John 10:27-28).

11. Pray for the child.
12. Encourage the child to talk to their parent/s about the step they have made.

Nothing compares to the moment a new baby arrives into the world. I can recall the three moments when our children arrived, vividly. Each one was so different, even though they were so tiny. Daniel arrived four weeks early, and was small enough to sit in the palm of my hand. Newborn babies are so vulnerable. They are completely dependent, and without the attention of hospital staff and the warmth and food provided by Mum, they would die.

In heaven, nothing compares to the spiritual birth of a new family member.

Chapter 5
Maternity Ward

Evangelism is never an end in itself. Spiritually, the life of the new believer is just as fragile and dependent as the newborn baby. They will need encouragement and feeding if they are going to begin to grow in their faith.

Just as we need stepping stones in place to bring children to a point where they can be brought into God's family, so we need to put stepping stones down for children to be integrated into the life of the church. The first of these could be a nurture group. Children Worldwide have a six-week children's nurture course, and this can be extended to deal with particular doctrines or practices that you might like to add.

What are the keys to running a successful nurture group?

1. Strike while the iron is hot. Get something going as soon as you have two or more children who will benefit from it.

2. A small group works best. Ideally six to eight children. If you have more, thank God, and then set up more than one group.

3. If possible use a home. This will provide the informal, relational setting that will work best.

4. Invite the children you want to attend. Do not make it open to anyone. This will not be a recreational club. It has the specific purpose of helping new believers to set off on

a good footing. You may want to invite children who have been in God's family for quite a long time, but whom you feel will benefit. Write a note to parents explaining what you plan to do.

5. Set the right time. Straight after school, or at about six o'clock when children have finished their tea. The club should last about an hour.

6. Give the group a name. In the past we have called ours 'Discovery Groups'.

7. Leave space to talk and review. Find out how the children are getting on with trying to put their faith into practice. Encourage.

8. The key to a lasting success is to train and not just to teach. We have a whole chapter on that coming up, so I will resist the temptation to go into detail here.

9. Give time to praying. Teach the children how to pray for each other, and pray for them yourself. God can do far more for them than you can!

10. Power phrase – teach the children a verse each week. '*The word of God is living and active*' (Hebrews 4:12). This way you are arming them against the enemy.

11. Praise and worship – have fun with some praise and worship. If, like me, you are not a musician, put a CD or tape on. The enemy hates to hear children praise! '*From the lips of children and infants you have ordained praise because of your enemies, to silence the foe and the avenger*' (Psalm 8:2). It is a good principal to get the children doing damage to the enemy before he tries to do damage to them. Don't make your praise and worship religious, keep it light, but real.

12. Review your teaching. Use a quiz game to review the teaching of previous weeks as well.

13. Run the group for a set period and then finish it. This is just a stepping stone into the other activities you run. We have run our course annually, normally after a holiday club.

The big question is what subjects to cover. These are the chapter headings in the Children Worldwide *Thank you Jesus Discovery Book*:

1. *Starting Out.* This is to look again at what happens when someone chooses to join God's family. It will remind the children of what they have done, and give them a chance to share their own account of it.

2. *The Bible.* Briefly setting out to explain what the Bible is, and why it is vital for us to feed from it.

3. *Talking with God.* Showing that prayer is more than talking *to* God, it is a two-way conversation. Some basic teaching on prayer which could be supplemented with trying some different ways of praying.

4. *Facing Problems.* Helping children to understand where problems and temptations come from, so that they are better equipped to overcome them.

5. *God's Family.* Looking at the church, and how we fit in.

6. *Telling Others.* Helping the children to understand the importance of witnessing with our lives as well as our lips.

The above will fit neatly into a six-week course, but we have added on the odd extra week to cover:

1. *The Holy Spirit.* Helping children to understand who he is, and how he can empower them to live for Jesus.

2. *Baptism.* Looking at how our own church baptises believers.

By the time Jake has made it through the Discovery Group, he is beginning to find his spiritual feet. His relationship with you and other Christians has deepened, and he has a much better understanding of what it means to be part of God's family.

The spiritual development of a child

Jake's doing fine, but what about Mike. He has grown up in a Christian home. His parents are Christians, and he can't remember when he joined God's family. He feels as if he has always been part of God's family. He envies Jake a little bit. Jake can tell you the exact day when he decided to join. Mike wonders if he really is a Christian or not.

Mike's problem is common to many children growing up in a Christian home. I can relate to it myself. Children like Mike seem to go through a process of conversion rather than coming to a dramatic conversion experience like the apostle Paul. So what is going on?

The Bible teaches that each one of us needs to come to a moment in time when we turn away from living for ourselves, and receive Jesus as our Saviour. This is just as true for Mike as it is for Jake. We have already seen that there has been a journey for Jake to get from where he was to where he is. Mike's journey has been different. God has been a part of his life since his birth, but there have been some important landmarks in the journey. Let's look at the spiritual development of a child growing up in a Christian environment.

Before birth

Warm, dark and safe, the womb is the place where children become conscious. They begin to hear the outside world. Their welfare is tied up with their mother's – quite literally. Repetitive sounds become familiar: the signature tune of that soap opera Mum has been watching during her pregnancy, Mum's voice, and the voices of the rest of the family.

Here they can begin to experience God's presence. Esther was born in April 1995. The previous year had been one of great excitement and blessing for our church. Esther spent many hours in an atmosphere of worship and receiving from God. I believe that this was a vital foundation stone in the relationship she had with God as an infant and into the early years of her childhood.

In one church in Nigeria the Sunday groups for children start with unborn children! Expectant mums have their own class, but it is not just for the mums. The class is provided so that the babies can be prayed for and can hear praise and worship that is planned with them in mind.

First impressions

However unusual a child's home is, to them it is the norm. Children growing up in a Christian home quickly pick up that God is a part of the family. His presence is not strange. The fact that people talk to someone invisible is never questioned. Children pick up the atmosphere and character of the home long before they can understand language. Their experience of God is deepened at bedtime if a Bible story and a prayer are included in the routine. My mother used to sing a lullaby as we went to sleep, 'Jesus tender Shepherd keep me'. It has affected my understanding of Jesus to this day.

And so the child begins a relationship with God. As soon as they can talk, they can pray. At this stage bedtime prayers are wonderfully chatty and informal. Sometimes as a parent it is difficult to know if the child is talking to you or God. It is as if there are two of you sitting on the bed, and one snuggled down with cuddly rabbit or teddy. God's presence is natural.

While the child is very young, they will learn to appreciate God's goodness and provision. They will learn that the family go to him for their needs, and seek him for the needs of others. He is the one who provides comfort in times of sadness. He is a heavenly Father.

Heart

In time the child comes to a point where they may wish to respond to God personally for the first time. In their own way they want to commit themselves to God. For me this happened when I was four, as I mentioned earlier. Very young children may want to make a personal response to Jesus at a holiday club or some other activity. What should we do? Should we say no, on the basis that they do not fully understand salvation, sanctification, and redemption? What did Jesus say? *'Let the LITTLE children come to me, and do not hinder them'* (Matthew 19:14).

Little children, that is pre-school children, can respond to Jesus. Their response is based primarily on their emotions. This first stage of their conversion is a conversion of the heart. They understand that God loves them and wants to care for them. They want to love him too. This love is immeasurably precious to God, as we saw in the first chapter. It is important that we respect and value this early step towards God as much as he does.

Head

Mike has got past this stage. He said a prayer asking God to accept him into his family when he was five, but something has happened to him at holiday club this year too. It was the story of the cross that got him. He had heard it many times before, but this time it really struck him, that Jesus had died for him personally. He had never quite seen it like that before. He felt God was speaking to him when the chance was given to go to the chat corner. So off he went. What should the counsellor have done? Should he have told Mike that he had already responded to Jesus, and was part of his family, so he didn't need to do it again? Should he have ignored the initial response and treated this as a first?

Children, who already have a loving relationship with God, will begin to understand in their minds what we need to do in response to Jesus' death and resurrection. They will understand for the first time that sin separates people from God. They will understand that the cross was all about Jesus being punished in their place. They will understand that they can be forgiven if they repent and ask for forgiveness. Suddenly it all makes sense.

So let Mike make a fresh response to Jesus based on what the Holy Spirit has revealed to him. This does not devalue Mike's first response years earlier, or mean that his relationship with God has been a sham. It is just the next step in his journey.

Psychiatrists tell us that by the time a child is seven they have learned half of all they will learn in a lifetime. This is a staggering thought. Primary-aged children soak up knowledge like a sponge. This is a key time for teaching and training.

Hands

For many young people there is a third stage to the process of conversion. Ideally this stage should come with the second, and we will look at why it doesn't in the next chapter.

Mike is in his teens now. He is experiencing all the joys and traumas of adolescence. God is real to him, but he still feels there is something missing. He listens intently as the speaker challenges people to live for God. 'You can be a Christian, and still not live for Jesus,' says the preacher. Mike knows that is him. He feels frustrated, and disappointed with himself. He has committed his life to Jesus, but he knows he is not living for him. His life is just about the same as everyone else's in his year at school, accept he gets dragged along to church services on Sunday. The fun has gone out of his relationship with God. Slowly he makes his way out to the front in response to another appeal. 'You have my heart, and my head,' he prays quietly. 'Now take my hands. I want to live for you'. For me this stage coincided with someone praying for me to receive a fresh filling of the Holy Spirit. I wonder if this had not happened whether I would have seen a real change in my life, but thanks to the grace of God, I did.

Unlike Jake's experience, Mike's has been a long process of conversion. 'Where', you might ask, 'was he born again?' I don't know for sure, but God does, and that's all that matters.

Chapter 6

Making Disciples

Next Sunday, 1000 children will attend church for the last time. There is a rapid decline in the number of young people attending churches. The main area of concern is among eleven to fifteen-year-olds, since this is the age at which so many young people drift away from the church.

The decline is alarming. This at a time when there has been a great movement towards praying for revival. Can anything be done to reverse the trend?

In the last two centuries children's work has been deeply influenced by a Sunday school mentality. Sunday schools were started by Robert Raikes, as a way of reaching children who were not getting a proper education. He was born in Gloucester in 1736, and learned the art of becoming a newspaper editor from his father, who founded the *Gloucester Journal*. Robert Raikes was deeply affected by a prison visit he made. Many of the inmates were there for taking part in a riot against the price of grain. The conditions in the prison were appalling and he set out to use his position as editor, which he had inherited on his father's death, to highlight the plight of the prisoners.

Raikes was also concerned about the plight of the children that he saw on the streets of Gloucester. Most of the children had no education, and worked in the pin-making industry for six days a week. Raikes noted that on Sunday 'the street was full of children cursing and swearing and spending their time in noise and riot.' He made a connection between those early childhood years and the prisoners he had seen, recognising that their lives had been shaped by their experiences as children. This gave birth to the idea of starting a Sunday school, a place where children could gain a basic education in a Christian environment. He hoped that this would give them a chance to break out of the cycle of poverty and crime that trapped them. The first Sunday school was opened in Sooty Alley opposite the prison in 1780.

The idea caught on and soon there were many other Sunday schools. By 1785 the Sunday School Society was formed to coordinate the rapidly growing movement. And in just five years attendance in Manchester had grown to 1800. A similar number were attending in Leeds.

Children from five to fourteen were admitted (later the age group was widened, and even included adults). Lessons were given by suitable ladies who were paid one shilling and six-pence. ('Hey! I don't get paid,' I hear you cry.)

Amazingly, even after more than 220 years, our children's ministry is still deeply influenced by the legacy of the Sunday school movement, even though conditions have changed drastically, and children receive their education from the State. The most obvious indication of this legacy is that our current Sunday schools are still primarily teaching based, rather than training based.

Now, Sunday schools have become closely linked to Sunday services, often running parallel to them. At worst, Sunday schools are an excuse for marginalising children and keeping them on the edge, just as the disciples did. Children are always 'taken out' of the service, which is seen to be the centre of worship, to go to their groups, which may be in a cold back room.

The main problem though is that many children find the gap between what they are taught on a Sunday morning, and what they experience at school on Monday morning is too big.

Our emphasis needs to change rapidly away from a teaching-based model, to a training-based model.

Teaching has to do with imparting knowledge.

Training has to do with providing experience.

While training is not possible without teaching, teaching is ineffective without training.

I believe the best model for children's ministry is that described in the Gospels. It is the model that Jesus himself used to disciple his disciples. It is a training model.

Let's look at the principles that Jesus used, and see if we can use the same principles to build a strategy for our own children's ministry.

Be warned. If you read on, it might turn your kids' work upside down!

So you want to go on! Well, here goes . . . Jesus told his followers to '*go and make disciples of all nations*' (Matthew 28:19). After that he left them to it. Well not quite, because the Holy Spirit came a short while later to empower them. But Jesus had completed his training. His disciples were equipped to face anything. How did he do it?

First, how he didn't do it. He did not do it by having a weekly Sabbath Class. His disciples lived with him for three years. He did it by training them.

The idea of living with your Sunday school class for three years may not seem immediately appealing, but let's see if we can look in some detail at how Jesus went about discipling his disciples. Is there a pattern we can apply to our own ministry?

Jesus called his disciples

There is something magnetic about the person of Jesus. Who else would get the response he gets as he walks along the beach calling to first Simon and Andrew, then James and

John. These no-nonsense fishermen simply drop their nets, leave family behind and fall in behind the Master. Even Matthew the tax collector leaves his lucrative booth to follow Jesus. His arrival will go down like a lead balloon with the fishermen! A tax collector working in tandem with the Romans! Then there's the other Simon who belongs to the Zealots. They are an organisation regularly involved in terrorism against the Romans! What a mixed bag Jesus had chosen. In each he saw potential for the kingdom of God.

We do not generally choose the children we get to work with! Jesus did choose. But I have come to the conclusion that God chooses the children that he brings under our care. Each child is entrusted to us, and God has a reason for them being in our care. There may be days when you hope a certain child or children will not attend – but sure enough they turn up like clockwork, while others you want to keep may drift away. Understanding that each child in our group is there because God wants them to come under our ministry gives a sense of purpose and hope. Begin to ask God what it is that God wants you to impart to each child he has given you.

As we begin to disciple children, we need to recognise that, just like Peter, they too have a calling on their lives. The calling is God's calling and not ours, but we have a role to play in identifying that sense of calling in our children. This has been a challenge to me over recent months, and I have asked God to begin to help me communicate that sense of calling to the children I work with. This is more than just telling them that God has a purpose for their lives, it is seeing with spiritual eyes, and beginning to encourage the children by recognising natural and spiritual gifts that God wants them to use.

Jesus did this with Peter. He didn't just ask Peter to follow him, he added that he would make him a fisher of men. He changed Peter's name from Simon, because his new name was tied up in his destiny.

Many children growing up in a Christian environment have had prophetic words spoken over them as babies, perhaps when they were christened or dedicated. Sometimes these provide another key to the calling on that child's life. Parents will probably have them treasured in their hearts or written down somewhere. It may be helpful to ask them.

My grandfather, Singleton Fisher, was a pioneer missionary in Central Africa. Sadly, he died when I was a toddler, so I don't have clear memories of him. Before his death he prayed over me, asking God to use me to reach others with the gospel. Years later God has led me into a ministry where I am able to do just that. I don't remember my grandfather's prayer, but the memory of it has been passed down to me through my parents, who felt that it was a calling on my life. I thank God that he searched for that calling in me when I was only four years old.

Other children come into God's family with no apparent Christian heritage. God has called them as surely as anyone else. We can begin to ask God to show us what that calling is so that we can encourage these children to press on towards the goal God has for them.

Jesus taught his disciples

Lessons for life

The Sermon on the Mount came close to the beginning of Jesus' ministry. It is true that he had already spent time teaching in Galilee, and that his fame had spread down to Judea, across the Jordan river, and up into Syria, but most of the training his disciples would receive was still ahead. Jesus begins his ministry with a wonderful teaching session. He is not teaching the people the Law or the Old Testament. The people got enough of that from the rabbis. Jesus was applying the teaching of the Old Testament in a radical new way. What he had to say really had an effect on people's lives then and there. He taught about murder, hatred, adultery, divorce, revenge, love, enemies, and the poor. Without this the disciples would have had no foundation on which to live their own lives, let alone teach others.

Good teaching is important for our children if they are to become effective disciples. They need to know their Bibles well, to be able to find their way around what is after all a library of sixty-six books, and to get a basic overview of the history of God's people.

I use the midweek children's club I run to systematically teach my way through the Bible. We spend two years in the Old Testament, and a year in the New Testament. So often our Bible teaching is haphazard, and children never get the complete picture of the story of the Bible. Maybe this is true for adults too.

Just as the disciples needed lessons on life issues, so do our children. This is one way in which we can begin to pull away the branches that lie in their paths.

Jesus' Sermon on the Mount was straightforward teaching, though the subject matter may well have ruffled a few feathers. It was laced with humour too. Whoever heard of someone with a log in their eye?

For a lesson about life issues to be well taught, there needs to be time for discussion. Ask the children who they consider their enemies to be. How do they become an enemy? How does God expect us to behave towards them? Teaching on its own will go in one ear and out the other. Discussion is the first step between teaching and training, and teaching your children to listen to each other is the second step.

I often sit the children in a circle of not more than twelve. We pass an object around the group. When each child receives the object it is their turn to speak if they want to. Nobody is allowed to speak unless they have the object. This teaches the children to listen to each other. At other times we have a more open discussion, but it still has to be carefully managed.

Telling Tales

On other occasions Jesus used stories as the foundation for his teaching. In Matthew 13:34 we read *Jesus spoke all these things to the crowd in parables; he did not say anything to them without using a parable.'*

Jesus knew the value of story telling. Today stories are still a wonderful way of helping children grasp abstract concepts from forgiveness to faith, redemption to restoration.

A story is something concrete. It can be visualised; it has characters that people can relate to, sympathise with, love and hate. A story can make a point very powerfully.

The prophet Nathan knew this when God sent him to have a little chat with King David. David had sinned. Lusting after Uriah's wife, he had sent Uriah to a part of the front line where he knew he would be killed in battle, and then he had taken Bathsheba to be his own wife. Nathan decided to tell a story:

> The Lord sent Nathan to David. When he came to him he said: 'There were two men in a certain town, one rich and the other poor. The rich man had a very large number of sheep and cattle, but the poor man had nothing except one little ewe lamb that he had bought. He raised it, and it grew up with him and his children. It shared his food, drank from his cup and even slept in his arms. It was like a daughter to him.
>
> 'Now a traveller came to the rich man, but the rich man refrained from taking one of his own sheep or cattle to prepare a meal for the traveller who had come to him. Instead he took the ewe lamb that belonged to the poor man and prepared it for the one who had come to him.'
>
> David burned with anger against the man and said to Nathan: 'As surely as the Lord lives, the man who did this deserves to die! He must pay for that lamb four times over, because he did such a thing and had no pity.'
>
> Then Nathan said to David, 'You are the man!'
> (2 Samuel 12:1-7)

Point made!

David can make no other response than *'I have sinned against the Lord'* (2 Samuel 12:13).

Time after time Jesus used a parable to get his point across.

The Unforgiving Servant shows how petty our unforgiveness is when held alongside all we have been forgiven by God.

The parable of the Lost Sheep illustrates the value of a spiritually lost child.

The parable of the Good Samaritan shows the power of loving your neighbour especially when they are supposed to be an enemy.

The parable of the Sower illustrates how easily we let the word of God get choked from our lives. In each case the story adds weight to the point.

There are two kinds of story in the Bible:

1. *Parables.* All the stories we have identified have come into this category. A parable is a story that is made up to get a point across.

   We tend to think that parables are limited to the Gospels, but there are parables dotted through the Old Testament too. We have looked at one. There is another in Judges 9:7-15. Can you find any more?

2. *Historical Events.* The stories of Zacchaeus or Lazarus are events that actually took place. Although there is much to learn from these stories, they are not parables, but historical events.

It's important to identify which kind of story we are telling, so that we can handle the story correctly when we tell it. Parables are often modernised, particularly when they are dramatised, so that the point can be applied in a setting more relevant to the audience. For historical stories a Bible atlas and commentary will help the storyteller to find out as much as possible about what actually happened, and what the culture and geography were like at the time. For example, Zacchaeus lived in Jericho, which is deep in the Jordan valley. It is very hot and dry there, so sycamore trees do not grow very tall. This factor was definitely in the favour of our diminutive tax collector.

Bible stories are a foundation in a child's spiritual growth. They are like a deposit that can be built on later. When Jesus told the story of the sower in Matthew chapter 13, he did not give the application to his audience. The disciples came to him later and asked him for the meaning of it. Why did he not apply it to everyone? Jesus makes it clear that the people are not ready to understand the meaning of the parable. God has chosen only to reveal it to the disciples. Months or years later, when this parable was read or retold, the same people, having heard Jesus tell the story, would have heard its application.

The full meaning of a story may not be fully understood by the children you tell it to, but a lifelong foundation will have been laid.

Look and learn

The third method that Jesus used for teaching his disciples was to provide an example. Being a disciple was not an academic exercise. It was a complete way of life. So much of what the disciples learned was not the finer points of the Law, but how to react when faced with a leper dying from his terrible condition, what to do when faced with bereavement, how to react when God's house is being used as a market place. None of this could have been done in the Sunday school room. The disciples learned through watching, which leads in nicely to the third stage in Jesus' 'Making Disciples' course.

Jesus demonstrated to his disciples

Time to say goodbye to Robert Raikes. This is where we begin to move away from the traditional approach to children's ministry. Teaching and story telling are familiar, but now we are moving into new territory.

A warm sunny morning, crowds of people squashed together. Sitting on rocks, on the grass, up trees, anywhere, as long as it was close enough to hear. *'I tell you, love your enemies and pray for those who persecute you'* (Matthew 5:44). Jesus' words rang out across the crowd. This was a hard teaching. What had happened to revenge? Jesus might have left the subject there, but would the disciples have understood the lesson?

Less than three years later, the disciples watched as Jesus wept over Jerusalem, hours before he was arrested. His love for that great city's people was very evident. These were his enemies. As the nails tore through his hands, and the soldiers mocked him he cried, *'Father, forgive them, for they do not know what they are doing'* (Luke 23:34).

The disciples had heard Jesus teach the principle of loving your enemies, now they could see it in action. Some of them would one day face similar persecution. Peter at least would face crucifixion.

To apply Jesus' example to our own ministry among children will be a real challenge. It will mean spending time with our children outside the church building. It will mean finding ways of spending time in their world to be an example for them to follow. It will mean being more transparent and honest so that they can learn from my mistakes.

One of the many ways I differ from Jesus is that Jesus did not make mistakes. His disciples learned by copying his example. I do get it wrong, and I don't want my children to copy my mistakes. But God can even use my weakness to his advantage. My children can learn from my mistakes, if I am brave enough to expose them. An incident happened recently that really brought this home to me.

We had been looking at the subject of witnessing with our children. In a later section, where we will look at some practical training ideas, I will go into some detail of what we did. In our midweek club we all prayed that God would give us an opportunity to witness in the week ahead. Sam aged nine took the training to heart, and wore his witness bracelet into school. When his teacher asked if anyone had brought anything into school to show the class, he raised his hand, and proceeded to explain the gospel to his teacher and class. Sam is normally quite shy. The teacher was so impressed that she asked if she could borrow Sam's bracelet to explain the Christian faith to the next class.

That same week I was in Sheffield city centre with an hour to kill. A young homeless man sat on the bench beside me and asked for some money. I got chatting with him. I found that he had just come out of court where he had been in trouble for shoplifting. Now he wanted to get home, and was looking for a coach ticket. I did not want to give him money to spend on drink, and I did not have enough money on me to buy a coach ticket, so I bought him a sandwich and we continued to chat. I was wearing my witness bracelet, and yet I said nothing to him about Jesus. As I was going home, I remembered our prayer, and I felt that I had missed an opportunity that God had given me.

Listening to Sam's story at club that Thursday served to underline my own shortcomings, which I shared with the rest of the group. God had answered our prayer, and given us an opportunity to witness. Sam had taken his opportunity, and I had missed mine.

Both our testimonies had the potential for helping the rest of the children. Sam had undoubtedly encouraged the rest of the group to believe that they could share their faith – just as he had done. But most of the children could not pinpoint a time during the week when they had shared their faith. Understanding that I get it wrong sometimes and want to trust God for another chance, gives hope to the children. If I give them the impression that I have got a perfect Christian life, I will only distance myself from them. They will feel that being a real Christian is something unattainable for them, and they will be inclined to give up.

Big Brother

This brings us to another hugely important question. What kind of relationship do I have with my children?

We have seen that the Sunday school model has affected the content and format of our children's ministry, but it has also affected the way we relate to our children. We are teachers, and they are students. If this is how we see our relationship with our children, we are unlikely to share our weaknesses with them in the way I have just described. 'Leave your problems outside the classroom,' I was taught in my early years as a children's worker. Now, more often than not I am taking them with me – not for my own gratification, but so that the children can pray for me and share with me.

In the Gospels, there is a real sense in which Jesus and his disciples are fellow adventurers. Experiencing the storm on the lake together, this time Jesus is the strong one. He stands up and rebukes the storm, and his disciples are gobsmacked, to use a contemporary phase! The situation is different in Gethsemane. Here the spiritual and emotional pain is almost overwhelming, and Jesus is desperate to share the moment with his disciples, and to draw strength from their prayers, but they let him down and fall asleep.

Jesus is not just a teacher for his disciples, there is something much deeper about his relationship with them. Later in the book of Hebrews, the writer captures the essence of this relationship in a phrase: *'Jesus is not ashamed to call them brothers'* (Hebrews 2:11).

We have already looked at the idea of new Christians being adopted into God's family, and seen that this is a biblical idea. If we take this on a step further, things become clear.

Spiritually we have a Father. He is God. When we repent and receive his forgiveness we can become adopted into his family. This makes every committed Christian a child of God. That means that I am God's child, and every believing child I work with is also a child of God. We are of the same spiritual generation, and Jesus is not ashamed to see himself as part of this same spiritual generation. He recognises that he has the same Father as me! That makes Jesus my brother. We could explore a whole chapter on what it means to have Jesus as my brother, but that would take us away from the point I want to make here. I am no more or less than a brother or sister to each believing child in my care.

Understanding this has had a dramatic effect on the way I relate to the children in my care. I am not a father to them, or an uncle. I am just a big brother.

I watched intrigued as my youngest daughter sat patiently under the tuition of her older sister as she taught her to draw. There is something very special about learning within that relationship. Something I do not have as a father.

Now if I can just learn the lesson of being child-like, I will be ready to serve God in the way that he loves.

Children look up to a big brother or sister in a way that they do not look up to an adult. There is no generation gap, just a recognition that the older sibling has more life experience. The younger sibling wants to be like the older one. God, make me a big brother to the children I work with.

Jesus apprenticed his disciples

As the disciples watched Jesus put into practice the lessons he had taught, they began to build up their own confidence. Now they were ready to begin to have a go themselves.

What a day it had been for Jesus. In the morning he had heard the devastating news that his cousin John had been killed in very unpleasant circumstances. In his grief he wanted to spend time alone with his Father, but the crowds were building up again, and there seemed to be no escape. He tried crossing the lake with his disciples to get away, but as soon as they arrived, they found that the crowds had followed them. The sun had set, and night had come before Jesus could be on his own. The disciples had been sent ahead to take the boat back across the lake, and to make things worse a storm was blowing up. As the storm reached its crescendo, the disciples found themselves in a life-threatening situation. Jesus had taught them about faith, he had demonstrated how faith works in the many miracles he had performed, now it was time to see how well the disciples could put faith to work. To add to the excitement a ghostly figure was seen walking across the mountainous waves. The faith of the disciples rose to meet the challenge? No, it sank as fast as their boat would sink if someone didn't do something quick! The disciples were terrified! Just as they thought all was lost, Jesus called to them, '*Take courage. It is I. Don't be afraid*' (Matthew 14:27). In the presence of Jesus they felt a little more confident, so Peter asked if he could have a go. While his eyes were on Jesus, the water held his weight, but when he looked at the waves he began to sink. Jesus reached out and pulled him up again, with a gentle rebuke.

There are other examples of Jesus encouraging his disciples to put into action the things they had seen him doing, like a mother bird encouraging her fledglings to take that first harrowing flight out of the nest.

The next step in the discipling process is to apprentice. This goes beyond demonstrating and setting an example. It means giving our young disciples a chance to begin to put into practice some of the things they are learning.

For a number of years our church has regularly got involved in 'servant evangelism', a phrase that puzzled Hannah when she was about five years old. 'Daddy,' she asked me once, 'what is servant vandalism?' Servant evangelism is simply doing small acts of kindness in the community as a demonstration of God's love. We have done all sorts of different things. At Christmas, everyone wraps up small gifts marked 'child', 'woman' or 'man'. Then on two Saturdays before the big day we go to where people congregate and give them away. There is a small card with each gift which says – 'This gift comes with love from the Oaks Community Church as a demonstration of God's love.' It really is very simple. Thousands of gifts are given away and the children enjoy getting involved. Many people are happier to receive a gift from a child than they are from an adult, and some people are very moved. Each year one or two people ask for prayer for some personal need. Some people react in the opposite way, refusing to accept something they are not being asked to pay for (that sounds familiar!). This is a good example of apprenticing. The children are getting involved with the adults and learn through doing. A prayer time and debrief afterwards gives everyone a chance to take stock of what God has done, and what they have learned.

Other servant evangelism activities have included: giving roses to ladies on Valentine's Day; giving away cream eggs at Easter; washing cars or car windscreens; giving away light-bulbs on people's doorsteps; cutting hedges; mowing lawns; or even cleaning toilets along a row of shops. Some of these activities are more suitable for children than others, but the principle is to look at where children can fit in and get them working alongside an adult.

Apprenticing is a vital part of training. Whenever I can, I like to take a child with me if I am going to take a meeting. This gives them a chance to experience different kinds of churches from our own, and to get involved through praying, reading, ministering to people at the ends of meetings, giving a testimony, or just helping to carry visual aids in and out of my car.

One half term, instead of running a holiday club, we ran a programme called Splash. It included recreational activities like a visit to the swimming pool, but also a community project where we cleared up all the litter from the valley behind our church. Armed with litter pickers and appropriate clothing, the clear-up was enjoyed even more than the swim, and we were trying to put a biblical principle into practice. The boys outdid each other to see who could haul out the biggest piece of junk. The children are less likely to be among those who deposit litter in the valley, now that they have cleared up. They are developing some ownership of the local environment, and an interest in keeping it clean.

Now we begin to see how vital are the earlier stages of this discipleship process. I can't expect a child to stand up and give a testimony unless they have been taught how to do it. Equally there is no point teaching them to do it unless they are going to have an opportunity to share it. The classroom may not be the best place to share your testimony first time! In this case we give children a chance to share testimonies in the safety of our Thursday evening club first. They sometimes do this in pairs, just chatting to a friend, and sometimes they will share with the whole group. They are being trained to the point where they will feel confident to chat with their friends at school, but it takes time.

What areas of your church's ministry would provide good apprenticeships for your children?

Jesus sent his disciples out in pairs

The day of the disciples' field trip had arrived! Jesus' next step in his school of discipleship is to get them into pairs and send them out into the world to practise without the Master at their side.

They are sent into the local towns and villages to preach, heal and release people who are in spiritual bondage.

It is worth noting that just before Jesus did this he spoke to them about the desperate need for more workers in the harvest field. *'The harvest is plentiful, but the workers are few. Ask the Lord of the harvest, therefore, to send out workers into his harvest field'* (Matthew 9:37-38). This is a risky prayer to express. The disciples ended up being the answer to that prayer themselves.

Our children often find themselves living and working in places where we cannot apprentice them, simply because we cannot physically be with them. In these places they will find strength in having a Christian partner. It is easier for them to see school as a mission field in the company of a friend than to try to live for Jesus on their own, in what can be a very hostile environment.

We can help this process by identifying children in our groups that live in the same area or attend the same schools. Pray for them in twos or small groups, and help them have a mission strategy for their school or class. We have two girls who were praying for their school in break times when they were just six years old. Who knows what has been achieved through their prayers?

There were clear instructions for the disciples as they went off on their short-term placements:

1. Have a clear idea who you are being sent to. Jesus told the disciples not to go to the Gentiles, but to the *'lost sheep of Israel'* (Matthew 10:6).

   We need to help our children to know who they are called to witness to and pray for. Maybe start with a limited number of people. Help them to be specific about what they are praying for.

2. Jesus told his disciples to mix words with actions. *'As you go, preach this message: "The Kingdom of Heaven is near." Heal the sick, raise the dead, cleanse those who have leprosy, drive out demons'* (Matthew 10:7-8). I have not had the courage to use these exact words with our children yet,

though I know, in times of revival, God has done wonderful miracles through children! I long and pray for a day when Christian children will have a miraculous ministry like this in their schools. Salvation would follow a demonstration of God's power and revival would break out.

So how do we apply this to our children? Jesus wanted people to see the kingdom of God lived out by his disciples. Their words were to work in harmony with their lives. This is how he wants all of us to live.

Actions speak louder than words, and Christian children will be watched and noticed by their peers. They, like us, are called to show Jesus in their lives. This may mean befriending children who are ostracised by the rest of the class, or not joining in with the latest craze in the playground.

3. Jesus prepared his disciples for opposition. *'I am sending you out like sheep among wolves'* (Matthew 10:16).

This is a good description of any child who is sent to school with instructions to witness for Jesus. School is about as tough a place as you can find to witness. Adults may disapprove of your faith, but they will tend to be discreet about their feelings. Children can be very cruel to any other child they consider different. We do our children a disservice when we put over the idea that joining God's family will solve all their problems, and give them an easier life. This is simply not true. Life will certainly be fuller, and should be more exciting and positive. The Holy Spirit strengthens and empowers us, but the reason we need the power is to enter into the battle that awaits us.

Many of the children who leave our churches are disillusioned. They are disappointed with themselves, and the Sunday school faith that bears very little relevance to the real-life situations they find themselves in.

We need to prepare our children for battle. We are not warning them of a life of doom and gloom. It is a glorious battle, that has already been won by Jesus, but it is none the less a battle. They need to know that their fight is not against flesh and blood, as Paul says when he writes to the Ephesians. Many children think that it is. They need to understand that it is God's enemy, Satan, who wants to do them harm. He is the enemy, not the children who bully them or even the teachers who dismiss their faith.

Perhaps the best way to prepare our children for the fight, is to take them to the dressing room in Ephesians chapter six. Perhaps it is no coincidence that the first word of this chapter is 'children'! There are instructions about being obedient to parents, but the section we are most interested in now is verses 10 to 18. We need to ask God to show us how to apply each piece of armour to the children we have, bearing in mind the specific battlefield they are preparing to fight on. Teach them how to mentally put their armour on. Give them a bookmark, or something they can take to school, that lists all the parts. Pray for them. Send them out as soldiers, not Sunday school children!

4. Jesus encouraged his disciples to expect the help of the Holy Spirit. *'Do not worry about what to say or how to say it. At that time you will be given what to say, for it will not be you speaking, but the Spirit of your Father speaking through you'* (Matthew 10:19-20).

To try to protect our children by suggesting they do not speak out for Jesus is to deny the ability of the Holy Spirit to help them. He promises to be there, and to give them the words to speak in difficult situations. He can accompany them when we cannot. We need to teach our children how to share the testimony of their conversion, if they can remember it, and how to talk about what God is doing in their lives now. They can practise this in their Sunday or midweek group.

Jesus reviewed their progress

'When the apostles returned, they reported to Jesus what they had done. Then he took them with him and they withdrew by themselves to a town called Bethsaida' (Luke 9:10).

Each pair of returning disciples would have had a different story to tell. Some would have seen miracles and repentance, others, opposition and hardship. Jesus knew that they needed to unpack their experiences and put them into context. Some would have needed encouragement and affirmation after entering into the battle.

Most adults take the opportunity to 'report back' what is happening in their lives in a cell group, or some other kind of small group. Here they can chat, and get the encouragement and prayer they need to press on. Christian children also need this kind of encouragement. A recreational midweek club does not usually provide the right environment for this, but a Sunday group, or children's cell or house group, can provide this vital service. If they don't get it their faith is likely to die, like the seed that fell among thorns and was choked.

We run a Friday evening discipleship school called Faith Academy. It is intergenerational, comprising children, teens and adults. Its purpose is to provide an environment where all of us can grow together in our Christian faith.

Sadly, many people think the Christian life mirrors physical human growth. There comes a time when we are grown up and don't need (or want) to grow any more. But God intends us to be more like crocodiles, that just keep on growing until they die! Faith Academy is for anyone – child or adult – who doesn't want to be the same in six months' time as they are now! The Christian life is a journey, but if we are to make progress along the road, we need pit stops to be revitalised, and to review the last section of road.

Where do your children have the opportunity to review their progress, and receive encouragement to press on?

Jesus commissioned them for service

Only three years bridged the gap between Jesus' walk along the beach calling his disciples to follow him, and the day he stood on the mountain giving his final instructions to them. Children seem to pass so quickly through our hands and into adolescence. We may only have three years to influence their lives. It is encouraging to know that Jesus was ready to leave his disciples after that same period. They were, of course, not left on their own. The Holy Spirit came to indwell them soon after Jesus had gone, and Jesus told them that his presence would be even better than Jesus' presence. The Holy Spirit would be inside them, not just beside them.

The last few verses of Matthew's Gospel are often known as 'The Great Commission'. There is an echo in Jesus' words from another earlier day when Jesus had sent out his disciples in pairs. But there is something more final about it this time. This is not going to be a short-term foray followed by a debrief. This is the real thing. Jesus will be leaving them to return to heaven and the Holy Spirit will come to help them.

> Then Jesus came to them and said, 'All authority in heaven and on earth has been given to me. Therefore go and make disciples of all nations, baptising them in the name of the Father and of the Son and of the Holy Spirit, and teaching them to obey everything I have commanded you. And surely I am with you always, to the very end of the age.'
> (Matthew 28:18-20)

While these are Jesus' last words, a more detailed commissioning takes place several weeks earlier as Jesus prepares his disciples before his crucifixion. The whole of John chapters 14 to 16 is a commission to the disciples.

The key thing is that Jesus wanted to prepare his disciples for what lay ahead. There was going to be a big change.

The big change for children is the move from primary education to secondary. It is a change that affects children very dramatically. They are moving from a relatively small environment where they are the oldest, and therefore setting the trends, to a huge environment where suddenly they are at the bottom of the stack. Attitudes are completely different. What you wear, what music you like, which jokes you laugh at, who you can be seen talking to, what you think of the opposite sex, and what you think of Jesus – all these things can be turned inside out. Peer pressure dictates a whole new way of life.

This change coincides with the plughole in our churches. This is when most of the 1000 children who leave our churches each week decide that church is no longer relevant to them.

This is why it is important that our children become strong disciples in their own right before they make the change. There is a real sense in which they need to be ready to be commissioned for the King's service before the move sweeps in on them.

When Steph and I finished college, my home church, Wickbourne Chapel in Littlehampton, arranged a commissioning service for us. It was an important landmark for us. We knew that the church wanted to own what we were setting out to do. They were with us. It helped to affirm our sense of calling, and helped us know that we were not alone.

Children need that same sense of support.

Am I making disciples?

It is clear from the words of Jesus that our commission is to 'make disciples' and not just converts. We need to stop what we are doing from time to time and ask ourselves this question. Am I, or are we, making disciples? Does our programme of children's activities achieve this end? Does the model I have identified make sense? Would it work for you? What changes would you need to introduce to make it work? How will your relationship with your children need to change?

We have looked at how Jesus trained his disciples. This gives us an excellent model to adapt for use in our kids' work. Training will help to prepare our children for those teenage years. Children who are taught but not trained are likely to struggle, and many will drift away from the church. Children who are trained and active in the church often display a passion for Jesus and for their lost friends which can be an inspiration to the rest of the church.

Chapter 7

Belonging

There is another important factor for us to consider in relation to keeping our children. They are far less likely to wander off if they feel they belong.

Belonging is an abstract concept. It is not easy to define in words, but we all know what it means. It is easy to identify the factors that add up to me belonging to my family. I am a dad, I have a wife and three children, but what factors help us feel that we belong to our church?

I used to visit a small chapel to take family services from time to time. Over the years I visited, the same child was always there to operate the overhead projector. His name was Carl. Carl was adopted into his earthly family, and though his new parents were sympathetic to the church, they did not regularly attend. Carl on the other hand was always there. He was the Overhead Projector Operator – quite a title! You soon found out that if you had acetates for songs or stories, you needed to liaise with Carl. Carl belonged. He felt he was an important part of the church; his job was what kept him coming.

When we first moved to the church that we now belong to and love, the leaders quite rightly gave us time to settle in. I found it really hard. We had been working for a church for a number of years, and were used to being right in the middle of everything. Now we felt as if we were on the edge.

There are three important keys that will help children (and anyone else) feel they belong.

1. Involvement

Congratulations, you have just taken up golf. You are a paid-up member of the local golf club, and this gives you the right to play whenever you wish. You have not, however, been invited to the annual members' dinner. You have some grounds to feel left out. Why did everyone else get an invitation?

If there are some things that are central to the life of our church that children are excluded from, this will enhance a feeling of not belonging! They are allowed to play, but they don't get invited to the members' dinner!

Looking at some of these activities will be controversial, but I believe it is essential to helping our children have a real sense of belonging:

a. *Membership*. How does someone go about becoming a member of your church? Can children be members? If they can't be members how do they get a sense of belonging? If they can't be members, we have nothing to complain about when they stop attending.

b. *Communion*. For many of us, Communion is central to our worship, and being allowed to take Communion is central to our sense of belonging. Can children take Communion in your church?

Is there anything in Scripture which teaches us that believing children should not take bread and wine? In the light of the value that Jesus puts on the belief of a child is it right for us to say 'no' to them?

We are in danger of doing what the disciples did. They separated the children by trying to keep them on the edge. This alienated the children, and put their faith into a different category from the 'adult's faith'. If we do this, we are refusing to share fellowship with our own precious brothers

124

and sisters. Jesus said: *'Let the little children come to me, and do not hinder them'* (Matthew 19:14).

c. *Baptism.* As I write, we are halfway through running a Preparation for Baptism class for children aged eight to thirteen. We use a number of criteria for assessing whether someone is ready to be baptised. We apply the same criteria regardless of age.

i.   Has the person taken the step of coming to God in repentance, and asked him to accept them into his family?

ii. Is there evidence of the person living for Jesus, and of Jesus living in the person?

iii. Have they asked for baptism of their own choice?

iv. Do they have a basic understanding of what baptism stands for?

If the answer to these four questions is yes, in the case of children there is one further requirement.

Do the child's parents agree to them getting baptised? In Scripture it teaches that children should be obedient to their parents, so where parents say 'no', we advise children to wait until they are eighteen. We would give the same advice to children from churches that say 'no' for the same reason. Obedience to church leaders is a clear requirement from Scripture.

Baptism can be a very important step in the life of a child who, like me, cannot remember when they were received into God's family. It gives a date and time that I can look back on. A time when I made a public declaration of my faith, and when the church was able to affirm me as a part of it. It helped me feel that I belonged. It still helps me feel I belong.

Apart from these big areas that believing children are sometimes excluded from, there are many smaller areas that children can get involved in that will help them feel they belong. Here are some examples:

1. *Taking part in meetings.* Being asked to pray, read, hold a visual aid. These are little things, but they all help. It will not only be the child at the front who feels they belong, the other children will feel a sense of belonging because one of them is involved. Why not get your children to plan and present a whole meeting?

2. *Having their names in the church directory.*

3. *Being invited to church members' meetings.* (Yes, I know they can be a bit fiery – perhaps the adults would behave better if children were present!)

4. *Communication.* The children should know what the main issues, aims and values of the church are. These need to be communicated to them in their language and in their pro-gramme. When a crisis arises – illness, or a prayer issue relating to an overseas missionary – communicating these things to the children will help them feel important enough to be included, and will give them an opportunity to get involved through prayer.

5. *Church Leaders.* Many children's departments are never visited by church leaders. This in itself says something to the children and their leaders about the value of children's ministry. It also means that children never get to meet the people who lead the church that we want them to feel they belong to. The leaders will do much to establish the char-acter and direction of the church, and it is important the children can begin to pick this up.

6. *Church Members.* When she was very small, Hannah once asked me if a certain lady in our church lived in the cup-board under the fire escape stairs in our church building. I suddenly realised that she had never seen this lady, who is

such an active member in our church, anywhere other than in our church building. Now we regularly invite church members to visit our kids' club and sit them in the 'hot seat'. I get a chance to ask them questions first, and then the children have their turn. Sometimes the questions need to be vetted, I confess, but since they still think 'What toothpaste do you use?' is the most embarrassing thing you can ask someone, I do not get too worried. We have found out ordinary things about people, like what they do for a job, their favourite food, their hobbies, as well as what Jesus has done in their lives. Usually we keep them long enough to pray for them. Our last guest was a South African pastor passing through our area, who has seen some fantastic miracles, including a lady who came back to life in one of his services! As you can imagine, the children had plenty of questions!

Some of the other areas where children can be involved will better come under key number two:

2. Responsibility

In Jesus' story of the talents there are three servants. Before the master goes away he gives five talents to one servant, two to another, and one to the third. The first two servants faithfully put their talents to work and double them, while the last one buries his one talent in the ground. It is interesting to note the master's response when he returns. His words to the first two servants are exactly the same: *'Well done, good and faithful servant! You have been faithful with a few things; I will put you in charge of many things'* (Matthew 25:21, 23). The master is not so much interested in how much he has got in return, but the fact that both men have doubled what they were given. Both are equally commended.

Children may well be represented by the second servant.

There is a limit to how much responsibility they can take on based on their limited experience, and the fact that they are still learning how to be responsible. They are not given five talents yet. God is just as pleased with a little responsibility taken seriously, as he is with a big responsibility taken seriously. His response is the same in both cases. The master seeing that the servant has been faithful commends them, and then gives them a little bit more responsibility.

This is an excellent example for us to follow in our children's work. Children will feel that they belong if they are given manageable responsibilities which they are helped to fulfil.

There are lots of starting points, but don't forget the principle. When someone is faithful in a small thing, give him a little more responsibility.

1. *Welcoming.* Put a child on your welcoming team and you kill several birds with one stone (if that's not an inappropriate analogy!). The child feels they belong because they have been trusted with a job. Any children arriving will feel that they are welcome because they see that children are taken seriously. Adults love to be welcomed by children.

2. *Collecting hymnbooks, stacking chairs, passing around biscuits* (without eating them all themselves!). There are a host of small routine jobs that children can do. Make sure that you are not asking a child to do something that could threaten their safety. Stacking chairs may not be safe for younger children. Pouring tea is not recommended for five-year-olds. Make sure that the children take their job seriously, and commend them if they complete the task faithfully.

3. *Overhead Projector, computer, digital projector.* Train up a Carl! Make sure the training is clear and effective. You want him to do a good job. Don't patronise him by just asking him to do it with no training, and then tolerate a sloppy job. Expect the job to be done to a high standard, and give further training if needed.

4. *PA Operator.* Operating mixing desks and microphones is a bit of a mystery to me, and I have great admiration for anyone who does a good job of it. This is an area where a child should not be left on their own, but it is a great area for apprenticing. A child can sit in alongside a designated adult and learn the ropes gradually.

5. *Prayer Team.* People wanting to become part of the prayer ministry team in our church are expected to complete some training, and then a church leader oversees them. Here is another great opportunity for apprenticing. Adults can be assigned a child buddy to stand alongside them when they are praying for people at the ends of meetings. There may be times when their 'adult' is praying for something personal, and it will be appropriate for the child not to be in attendance. They can sit down and pray for their adult a little way away. As we have seen, children have a much less cluttered faith when it comes to prayer for healing, and this is one area where sometimes they can take a lead. They will learn first from watching, then by praying with their adult, until they are able to take the lead in some situations. This is training not just teaching!

6. *Intercession.* This is another area of prayer. We were very moved to find out that children were part of the team praying for us as we were attending a children's ministry conference. Children who are trained to hear God, and to discern his purposes, can be a real asset to any intercession team.

7. *Planning Groups.* From holiday clubs to flower festivals, why not invite a child to be part of the group? It will bring freshness to the group, and train the child to become responsible whilst getting involved in a project that has a limited time scale.

8. *Worship Team.* When they can pray well enough, train your children to be part of the worship team.

There are, no doubt, many other areas where children can be

given responsibility while working alongside older brothers and sisters in Christ.

I am always excited to speak at Salvation Army Anniversary weekends, which I have done several times. I usually get to hear lots of different musical pieces performed, and it is so good to see children playing alongside adults. They have been putting these principles into action for generations. Here is a lesson for us all to learn.

My last word on this section though, is to say that this approach to training and belonging depends on the cooperation and attitude of the adults. The whole church needs to understand what you are trying to do. They need to get past seeing the children as cute or even a nuisance. This will mean the whole church being taught about the principles we are aiming to apply.

3. Environment and Programme

Some mornings I walk Esther down to her infant school. As we walk through the gate the playground greets us with its colourful wriggly snake, hopscotch grid and a wonderful wooden fort. Going into her classroom is like going into an Aladdin's cave. Granted, the gold is not solid, and the gems are children's paintings, but everything that meets your eyes says 'five-year-olds welcome!'. The chairs and tables are her size, and she knows every exciting nook and cranny in a classroom that is like a colourful maze. Esther feels she belongs there.

When children arrive at one of your meetings, what message does your building, or the building you use, convey? What is the child's experience as they walk in through the door? Do they feel they belong?

I'm not suggesting that every church building should be decorated like their local infant school, though adults might like the colour and excitement of it too! The way a church building is decorated and furnished will say something to the children about whether they belong. A child on the welcoming team, chairs the right height for legs not to have to swing, posters at a child's eye level, a children's cartoon on the notice sheet, or a video on in one corner before the service starts. All these things show children they belong. Sometimes we have a patch of floor at the front of our worship area that is free from chairs and we put gym mats down for children and parents to sit on. Valuing children's work, whether quiz sheets or pictures or things that they have written, will help them feel they belong. These can be mounted on the wall, but need to be looked after and changed. Perhaps one of the children can be responsible for this.

Making changes to the physical environment can be relatively simple. Preparing a service that is suitable for all is much more challenging.

Whenever children are expected to be present in a meeting of any sort, you have an all-age congregation and you need an all-age programme, or the children are going to feel marginalised. On a Sunday children are often expected to stay in to the first part of a meeting, and then go out to their classes. If children are going to feel they belong, the part of the service they are in needs to be planned with them in mind. This does not mean a selection of children's choruses. It is much better to find ways of making general worship accessible to the children, rather than choosing children's songs which may have the effect of marginalising and embarrassing the adults! We shall look at this in some detail under the knotty subject of all-age meetings. For the moment it is enough to suggest that when kids are present they should feel included.

Ideas for training young disciples

So here we go with some trade secrets. I would like to report that all our ideas work wonderfully, but the truth is that some of them work, and others don't! Such is the nature of trying new ideas. The ideas that follow have been used with our

Thursday evening group called Kool Kids, where our main aim is to train the children who attend to be strong disciples of Jesus. In many cases, we see our children developing closer relationships with Jesus, and going on to the next group for 11s to 14s without dropping away from the church. Our church also has a youth congregation with their own leaders, who meet once a fortnight. The worship style is more akin to a nightclub than a traditional service, and so there is something culturally relevant for our children to feed into.

Some of the children from Kool Kids do not come from Christian families, and we work hard to build relationships with these children for whom it is much more difficult to feel they belong. We always welcome new children, and actively encourage Kool Kids to invite their friends.

At Kool Kids we aim to provide a mixture of fun, friendship, letting off steam, creativity, and non-religious Christianity. We are not trying to realise unrealistic expectations in our children, or to push them beyond where God is taking them. We are not trying to make them into adults, but we do not want to limit God in the lives of our young brothers and sisters, so we want to give room for God to work.

Since our main principle in discipleship is to train rather than just to teach, we constantly ask ourselves the question; 'How can our children begin to put this subject into practice?' or perhaps more challenging; 'How can I begin to put this subject into practice with the children?' These ideas have in some way been the answer to these questions:

• How can we pray?

Some of the ideas we have used for prayer are included in the next chapter, so I will not go into them here.

News and prayer

One thing we regularly do just in Kool Kids is to have a 'News and Prayer' time. We meet all together or in small groups, each with at least one leader. Each person (child or adult) has an opportunity to speak. Sometimes we pass an object around the group so that when you are holding the object you know that it is your turn to say something if you wish. We have a firm rule that no one else is allowed to talk when you have the object, so that we can respect what each person has to say. Each person can share one or two things that have happened during the week, or mention someone or something that needs prayer. As soon as someone mentions an item that needs prayer we stop and ask someone else in the group to pray for that situation. If it is the child who needs prayer one or two other children may be encouraged to place a hand on their shoulder. On occasions we have kept a book of everything we have prayed for, so that we can write down the answer when it comes. This helps to build faith, and also to show that sometimes we have to pray for a long time before God answers.

Some years ago we prayed for a Russian pastor who was in prison for his faith. Each week we prayed, but instead of his release, we learned that when his sentence ran out it was going to be renewed because Alexander refused to promise not to preach the gospel. In the days before the collapse of communism our prayers seemed so futile in the face of the Russian Empire – to me that is. The children had faith that Alexander would be released. I was amazed one day to get a note through my door to say that Alexander had suddenly and unconditionally been set free. I expected the children to share my amazement, but while they were pleased they were not surprised. They had asked God in faith, and believed that his power was greater than that of the Russian Empire. It was only I that was surprised. Another lesson learned: children are good at praying for the impossible. God is good at doing the impossible.

More recently, one of the leaders asked us to pray for a lorry driver whose job was threatened because he was becoming increasingly unwell. The lorry driver was very moved when he heard that the children were praying for him, and wrote a very moving note to say thank you.

Prayer walking

Living in a small town on the edge of a big city, God has laid it on the heart of our church to pray for both. Sheffield is a city that was touched by revival in the days of John Wesley, and the many Methodist chapels in the area are the legacy of those days. We want our children to pick up a vision for praying for revival in Sheffield and Dronfield. The best way to do this is to physically go to the city. There are many key places to pray. We even persuaded the city council to lend us the city flag, which has flown over the city hall. The symbols on the flag offer more clues about the spiritual make-up of the city. Prayer and intercession for a city may sound like a complex and incomprehensible subject, but prayer walking can be fun, and helps children to begin to understand that there is a city that needs to be won for Jesus. Here are some things to think about if you want to have a go with your children.

Choose some key places to visit. Be realistic about how much time you will spend. Don't make the exercise too long. The children have shorter legs and smaller bladders than you!

We have a square called Paradise Square where John Wesley preached to his largest-ever outdoor, midweek crowd. The square still has its cobbles, and a brass plaque on a wall shows where Wesley once stood. What a great place to pray for revival! Are there places in your city, town or village where God has done a great work in the past?

We have a memorial set up in remembrance of a cholera epidemic when many died. From here you can see the hospital. This is a good place to pray for the sick.

There are places that represent commerce and employment, entertainment and education. All of these are key places to pray.

What gives your city its character? Where can you go to find a place that represents its character? This will be another good place to go and pray.

Sheffield is a hilly city, so there are high places with good views. In the Old Testament high places had particular spiritual significance. These were the places where things that were most highly revered were worshipped. Do you have a high place in your town?

When we set out we mix adults with children. We have found that children get on well with some paper and felt tips. The adults have prayed vocally, and the children have listened to what they think God is saying. They draw or write it down, which gives food for prayer back in the church building on Sunday or another club night.

There are plenty of good books on prayer walking. Read one and see how you can get your children involved. Be aware that when you do so, you are stepping onto a battlefield – literally. So make sure you pray for safety, and plan your outing carefully.

• How can we witness?

We have already seen that it is difficult for a child to share their faith. The playground can be full of spiritual piranhas. It is not good enough to tell our children the wonderful story of how Paul and Silas got beaten up at Philippi and thrown into prison, and then tell them that they too must go and witness for the Lord Jesus. They may get treated just as harshly. The beating may be verbal, and the prison may be exclusion from the rest of the class, but it is very painful just the same. So what are we to do? Shall we tell our children to keep their faith to themselves? I can't find a biblical mandate for that approach, so we had better try something else.

The training needs to start in the safety of the club, where there will be encouragement rather than discouragement.

From time to time we give our children the chance to give their testimony: to talk about how they came to be in God's family, and to talk about what God has been doing this past week. Many of the things the children want prayer for, and want to talk about, would seem trivial – the demise of a favourite guinea pig, a friend they have fallen out with, a school trip. But when they see God at work in these ordinary things, then you know that he is real in their lives.

Our key tool for witnessing is our witness bracelets. There is nothing new or unique about these, many people have used them before us, but we have got one that serves a valuable purpose. They are just leather thongs that tie onto the wrist or boot and carry six coloured beads. Each bead represents one aspect of the gospel:

Scarlet – Sin. *'Though your sins are like scarlet . . .'* (Isaiah 1:18).

See-through Red – Jesus Blood. *'The Son . . . in whom we have redemption through his blood . . .'* (Colossians 1:14).

White – Forgiveness. *'Wash me, and I shall be whiter than snow . . .'* (Psalm 51:7).

Yellow – Holy Spirit. *'He will baptise you with the Holy Spirit and with fire'* (Luke 3:16).

Green – Spiritual Growth. *'. . . we will in all things grow up into him who is the Head, that is, Christ'* (Ephesians 4:15).

Purple – Royalty. *'But you are a chosen people, a royal priesthood . . .'* (1 Peter 2:9).

The children love to wear these, and many adults in our church have bought them too, either to wear themselves, or to give to children.

Each child at Kool Kids is given their own bracelet, which we teach them to use. They learn what the colours stand for, and practise explaining the colours to a friend. Then they wear it whenever they can. If they want to, they can buy one to give to a friend. Each new one has a card with it that explains what the colours mean.

Many of our children have shared their faith using their bracelet, and some have led other children to make a commitment to Jesus.

Witnessing is more than just telling someone the basics of the gospel. It is a lifestyle, but at the core of the lifestyle, you have to *'always be prepared to give an answer to everyone who asks you to give the reason for the hope that you have'* (1 Peter 3:15). Our bracelets are tools to help children do this.

• What about injustice?

Children have a strong sense of justice and injustice, particularly when it involves themselves! 'It's not fair' is a phrase that is used by each new generation, and often thought by those who are older. Children also develop a strong sense of what is unfair in the world around them. They are concerned about other children in famine and war, and often get involved in sponsored events to help in whatever way they can.

Two of the children from my midweek club took it upon themselves to raise money to send a Russian girl to camp this summer. They decided to have a table-top sale, and pestered us to help organise it. In the end there was enough money to sponsor two children, and to give a gift to another appeal.

Caring about the global distribution of wealth is an important biblical principle that we want our children to understand.

Continental evening

One of our team worked hard to find out the average daily calorie intake for five different countries representing the five continents. The countries we chose were France, Mexico, USA, Morocco and Bangladesh. We asked parents not to feed their children any evening meal before Kool Kids one Thursday, and each child pulled out the name of one of the five countries from a hat. Thus allocated, we set about feeding them three good meals in the two hours they were with us. The children were seated in areas representing their country, and we made the rule that you could not ask for food from another country. Emotions rose high that evening. Children in the USA got sugar cereal and muffins for breakfast. The children in France got warm croissants and butter. The children in Bangladesh got water. Two boys in Bangladesh became very cross. One opted out and refused to take any further part. He sat in the corner for the rest of the evening. Things got worse at lunchtime when a beautiful chicken dinner arrived for the French children, burgers and fries followed by chocolate ice cream for the American children, and water and plain rice for the children in Bangladesh. By the third meal the children from the rich countries were stuffed with luscious goodies, and so overseas aid began in earnest. Relief came in from the USA and France, which was gladly received by most of the poor countries, except for the boy in the corner who was too angry to accept any aid. When we had finished we all got together to chat about what had happened.

'What did you think?' I asked.

'It wasn't fair,' replied one of the children from a rich country, a little embarrassed.

'How did you feel?' I asked the children from the poor countries.

'Angry,' they said.

'What if it was not just for an evening, but for a whole week?'

'What if it was not just for a week, but for a year?'

'What if it was not just for a year, but for a lifetime?'

Point made.

Homelessness

To help our children think through some of the implications of being homeless, we chose a dark evening in the autumn, got loads of old boxes from the local supermarket and dumped them in a pile in a large empty room. We would have done it outside, but it was raining! We left the lights and heating off and let the children build shelters for themselves. There were a few scuffles when it came to choosing the best boxes, but one or two children worked together to get comfortable. We talked about some of the problems that you would face if you really did have to sleep out on the street, and the children asked questions:

'Where do we get our food from?'

'How would we keep dry?'

'Where is the toilet?'

'How do you keep your things safe when you are asleep?'

'Are you allowed to sleep on the park bench?'

'Why don't people go home?'

Role play can help the issues become far more real. They help the children to step beyond teaching to experiencing, in a very small way, some of the issues that people really do have to face. On the Saturday after this exercise we took a group of children down into Sheffield to visit some of the places where people really do sleep, and to pray. It was still raining!

• Love your enemies

Each time we have a new subject to look at, we ask ourselves; 'What can we do to help our children experience this?' For loving your enemies we decided to make peppermint creams. These were put into carefully created baskets, which were decorated for the occasion. Then we asked the children to give them to someone who didn't like them. We explained that they were not to say, 'I am giving you these sweets because you are my enemy'! Instead they were just to give them away and say that they had made them to give away at Kool Kids.

I would like to report that all the children followed this

through, but some did not. Some children ate their own. Others gave them to a brother or sister they did not get on with or to someone at school. When we debriefed, the most commonly used word was 'gobsmacked'. The recipients couldn't understand why they were receiving a gift from someone who was not their friend. We thought about what Jesus had done on the cross.

• Mission

Here's another area that children can struggle with. Yesterday a little boy told me he had been to Eastbourne. He underlined this dramatic announcement by adding, 'It's at the end of the world.' When I asked him what he meant, he pointed out that the sea started at Eastbourne. How could there be anything beyond that? Distance is a relative thing. Young children think in terms of how far it is to the end of the garden, or as far as they can see. How can they understand the idea of a missionary working on the other side of the world?

To some extent the distance doesn't matter. It is important, however, for our children to learn about the mission links that the church has. If someone has been on the field for four years, your group of six-year-olds will not even remember what they look like. Here are some ideas for making a closer link between your children and your overseas workers.

1. *E-mail.* Sometimes all thirty Kool Kids pile into my office to send a message. One sits and types slowly and deliberately, while all the others shout instructions. Then off goes the message. It's great to find a reply within a day or two. E-mails tend to be more chatty and less formal than letters.

2. *Phone.* Kids love to talk to missionaries. They are intrigued by the difference in time, and can find out what is happening right then and there. If you are clever you can hitch the phone up to a sound system so that everyone can hear. If phoning is too expensive, text them.

3. *National evenings.* Role play a day in the life of your missionary. It would be great to take all the children with you to Guinea-Bissau or Timbuktu, but, failing that, do what you can to make Timbuktu come to you. It will help to have some items left by your missionaries on their previous visit, or to have some sent to you. Photos and slides are second best compared to objects you can actually get your hands on.

4. *Pen Pals.* Could some of your children write to children of a similar age living in the vicinity of your missionary?

5. *Support.* Children can learn to pray regularly for your missionary, and even to start to tithe pocket money towards their support.

6. *Home Mission.* Don't forget workers who are missionaries on your doorstep. Get them in for a visit, and talk to them. Are there other missionaries working in your town who could come and meet your children? A real live person is worth a hundred books.

Now it's over to you. How can you move from teaching to training? How can you take the children you work with and begin to learn with them? How can you make your next session an experience rather than a lesson? When you have worked out the answers, write a book and send me a copy!

Take a deep breath and get ready to look at another key to belonging.

Chapter 8
All-age Hot Potato

Time to juggle a hot potato! All-age meetings or family services are often the most difficult to lead, and can be the source of a fair amount of grumbling and huffing! No, I know none of these things happen in your church, but they do happen!

Why?

Would it be easier not to have them? Probably. So why should we have them?

A biblical model

In the Old Testament great occasions are marked by a coming together of all the people.

Solomon's temple is complete. The splendour of it is breathtaking. Now it is time for it to be dedicated to the Lord. He calls together all the people of Israel to participate in this great event: *'Then Solomon stood before the altar of the Lord in front of the whole assembly of Israel . . . '* (1 Kings 8:22). What a day. Solomon's prayer is still remembered 3000 years later. The king blesses the whole nation. It is not a good day for cattle, sheep and goats. Twenty-two thousand cattle and one hundred and twenty thousand sheep and goats are slaughtered! Messy! I don't think anyone forgot the occasion for a long time.

Josiah had become king when he was just eight years old. His life was dedicated to bringing his nation back to God. Now, at the age of twenty-six he had made funds available for the temple to be restored. In a dark dusty corner, long forgotten, a priest found an ancient scroll. It turned out to be the Law of Moses. It was God's word. Josiah called an all-age meeting: *'He went up to the temple of the Lord with the men of Judah, the people of Jerusalem, the priests and the prophets – all the people from the least to the greatest'* (2 Kings 23:2). This was a very different occasion to the opening of the temple. This was a time of getting right with God. Many wicked things were solemnly brought out of the temple and burned in a valley outside the city. The people pledged to turn back to God.

Many years later Ezra helped to lead God's weary people back from slavery in Babylon to Jerusalem. Once more God's precious word is brought out to read: *'Ezra the priest brought the Law before the assembly, which was made up of men and women and all who were able to understand'* (Nehemiah 8:2). There were even some actions for the first bit of worship! *'Ezra opened the book. All the people could see him because he was standing above them; and as he opened it, the people all stood up. Ezra praised the Lord the great God; and all the people lifted their hands and responded, "Amen, Amen!". Then they bowed down and worshipped the Lord with their faces to the ground'* (Nehemiah 8:5-6).

Many of the people had never heard the Law being read to them before. It was a part of their history, something they had whispered about when they were in exile, but now they were hearing it read for themselves. What an occasion: *'They (the priests) read from the Book of the Law of God, making it clear and giving the meaning so that the people could understand what was being read.'* A good example there for anyone who wants to lead an all-age service! Don't forget to explain things in a clear, nonpatronising way. An amazing thing happened as the Law was read. People began to cry, as they realised that they had not been following God's law. Some may have been crying for the joy of hearing God's word read after such a long time. Either way, the priests had to calm the crowd, and encourage them to rejoice. Repentance leads to rejoicing. The meeting went on all day. Many hungry people with tear-stained faces and weary legs trudged home that night. A new beginning had dawned in Israel.

Apart from these great landmarks in Israel's history, God's people were blessed with a whole range of feasts that were all-age occasions. From the Day of Atonement when sacrifices were made for sins, to the Feast of Tabernacles when children were involved in making a shelter good enough to sleep in. There was the Feast of Purim when they remembered how God had rescued them in the days of Esther – a day of joy, and feasting and giving of presents – and the Passover with all the excitement of acting out that night before the escape from Egypt. The feasts are full of action and interaction. There were elements that were experienced by all God's people as they came together as a congregation, and there were elements that were experienced in the home by family units; the children were always involved. They were not just looking on. There were things to hear, passed down from generation to generation, there were things to see, and taste and smell.

'Ah,' you say, 'but that was the Old Testament, there are no all-age meetings in the New Testament. We are not living in Old Testament times.'

The other way to look at it is that there is no record of people being segregated into age groups when the church came together to worship. It is true that Paul and Silas went to speak at a ladies' meeting when they visited Philippi, but that seems to be because at that stage no men had yet been converted. Perhaps the Philippian jailer was the first, and by the end of the night on which he was converted his whole household had joined God's family. The following Sunday might have seen the first real all-age service in Philippi.

Then there was Paul's visit to Troas. The believers met together to share bread and wine, and Paul was down to preach. Even he could not always keep his congregation awake all the time. We don't know what time he started to preach, but we do know that he was still going at midnight. *'Seated in a window was a young man named Eutychus, who was sinking into a deep sleep as Paul talked on and on. When he was sound asleep, he fell to the ground from the third storey and was picked up dead'* (Acts 20:9). The story has a happy ending though, as Paul performs a miracle and the young man is brought back to life. Most preachers would have packed in and called it a night at that stage, but not Paul. He broke bread with his congregation and then continued his sermon until daybreak.

Part of the body

When Paul writes to the Corinthians he describes the church as being like a body. Paul wants his readers to know that everyone is important to the body of Christ. Everyone has their part to play, and no one can say that they don't count. When we apply this to children, we see that their part is just as important as anyone else: *'God has combined the members of the body and has given greater honour to the parts that lacked it, so that there should be no division in the body, but that its parts should have equal concern for each other'* (1 Corinthians 12:24-25). I wonder who Paul was talking about when he referred to the parts that lacked honour?

Of course it is possible to have a united church without having all-age meetings, but there is a sense in Paul's teaching of the importance of functioning together. Surely this should include times when the whole church is together for worship.

Worshipping together

There is great benefit in learning across generations. We have looked at some of the ways we can learn from children, but children also need to learn from being in the presence of adults.

Training for family life

All-age meetings provide an environment where households can hear God and learn about Christian living together. This will provide a foundation for further discussion at home, where the family can think about a corporate response. Some of the ideas used in all-age meetings can be picked up and used in family times at home.

Children at the centre of church life

All-age meetings counter that feeling of always being 'sent out' from what is perceived to be the main event. Children also learn how to engage and behave through a whole meeting. This helps them to feel more integrated by the time they choose for themselves whether they are going to attend meetings or not.

Mentoring

If children do not worship with adults, there is no opportunity for them to be mentored in meetings. In all-age meetings children can learn to do anything the adults do. They can be part of the band, help to lead worship, work on the PA desk, read, preach, give testimony and pray. They can be a part of the ministry team, praying with people at the end of the meeting. Children who leave the meeting after twenty minutes may never hear a testimony, hear someone preach, or be present when people are responding.

All-age meetings: how not!

Perhaps one of the reasons we struggle to find a workable formula for all-age meetings is that historically they have done more to broaden the generation gap than to close it!

Family services have often been divided into items suitable for the children and items suitable for adults. There might be a hymn and a prayer (adults) followed by the notices (?) followed by a children's address (children) followed by a children's hymn or some choruses (children), followed by the children leaving for their classes. This will reinforce a sense of segregation rather than integration or belonging.

If you go to see a family film or visit the pantomime, the whole family becomes immersed in the fun. You can't identify different bits for different age groups. The whole appeals to everyone and boundaries are broken down as children and adults enter into the spirit of the occasion.

One of the problems with a segregated approach is that adults feel embarrassed when they are asked to be a 'fuzzy wuzzy bear', and children get bored when they have to sit through the 'adult' bits. I am not suggesting that adults should not enter into doing the movements for songs, but there is a difference between asking people to be childish, and child-like! I am not suggesting that children should not learn to sit quietly and listen sometimes, but if they are truly bored it is the fault of the programme or the presenter, not the child. The other point is that children, who are used to the latest pop group, feel patronised when they are asked to be fuzzy wuzzy bears. If not patronised, they will get the message that Christianity is old-fashioned.

Is it time to lay the traditional family service to rest, in favour of training up radical young disciples who will not dream of walking away from the church they feel they belong to?

All-age meetings: how?

In this section we will try to lay down some principles for all-age meetings. This is the easy part. Deciding what to actually include in an all-age meeting is the difficult part, and it will depend on the demographic make-up of your congregation, as well as the flavour of your churchmanship! Hopefully these principles can be taken and applied in a wide range of different church settings.

Underlying principles

See which ones you agree with!

1. Everyone is of equal value in God's eyes.

2. We recognise the spiritual potential of each person regardless of age, gender or position.

3. Spiritual gifts are distributed to believers regardless of age, gender or position.

4. It is unrealistic to expect that every item in an all-age meeting will meet the preference of every person, so there will often be times when *each of (us) should look not only to (our) own interests, but also to the interests of others'* (2 Philippians 2:4). This will mean that we will need to enter into the bits we least like for the sake of our brothers and sisters, and for the sake of the Lord Jesus.

5. The content should include something for everyone. Meat cut into small pieces, not just milk. The Bible is central to what we teach.

6. All-age meetings should not be too long.

7. Items within the meeting should not be too long. About eight minutes being the maximum for any one item.

8. Praise and worship should include songs and hymns for everyone. While some songs will be included that are particularly suited to children, the main emphasis will be

on songs suitable for everyone. Worship times can include creativity expressed in movement, art, and other media to make them accessible for children and adults.

9. Parents or guardians are responsible for the behaviour of their children before, during and after meetings. Now there's a subject to write a book about!

10. Parents or guardians are responsible for training their children to engage in the meetings.

11. All-age meetings should provide:
    - An opportunity for everyone to praise God.
    - An opportunity for those who love God to worship him.
    - An opportunity to learn about God.
    - An opportunity to hear from God.
    - An opportunity to pray to God.
    - An opportunity to interact with God's people.
    - An opportunity to respond to God.

12. Each meeting should include:
    - Things to see.
    - Things to hear.
    - Things to do.

All-age meetings: what?

So, having established some principles, what do we need to do to plan and present an all-age meeting?

1. Choose a theme

Working in my home church I will always ask God to show me what he is saying to the church at the time. Quite often there is already a current theme running through what God is doing in other meetings and church activities. I want the all-age meeting to be in tune with that.

When your theme is chosen try to put it into a few concise words, so that everyone involved can be quite clear what it is. It may also be helpful to identify the theme for the congregation at the start of the meeting by putting it up on OHP or digital projector.

2. Plan the praise and worship around the theme, but do not be tied to it

In the Bible there is a distinction between praise and worship. The last verse in the book of Psalms reads: *'Let everything that has breath praise the Lord,'* (Psalm 150:6). Praise is something that God requires from his whole creation. Worship can only come from people who recognise the Lordship of Jesus in their lives.

It can be helpful to keep this distinction in mind when we are choosing songs, and sometimes it may be helpful to separate the worship from the praise in the programme.

It is common practice to leave the 'message' to the second half of the meeting, but sometimes the theme will suggest that the message comes early in the meeting and praise and worship comes out of it. If the theme is 'Saviour' for example, you may want worship to follow what is said so that people can sing about Jesus having already heard about him. The worship will be even more meaningful.

Another benefit of having your message early, is that the younger children will be fresher, more likely to take in what is being said and less likely to fidget.

Praise and worship can be expressed in many ways other than just singing. The more variety and choice there is, the more likely it is that everyone will join in. Here are some ideas we have tried:

a. *Instruments.* One of our leading musicians has worked hard to mentor and train children with musical ability in our church, so that several of them often play in the band, and not just at all-age meetings. Others have learned to sing into mics to help lead the worship. One of our worship leaders is a teenager.

Other children are encouraged to bring percussion instruments that they can join in with. We have guidelines for parents so that they can help their children to know when to use them, and when not to use them. Sometimes there are moments of quiet or songs that would be spoilt if someone is banging a drum, so the instruments need to be carefully regulated. All-age services can be 'messy'. The children do not always behave appropriately, and this requires patience and understanding from the more mature members of the congregation.

b. *Flags, Ribbons and Creative Arts.* These can add colour, life and movement in times of praise and worship, and adults love to have a go as well as children. Empowered by the Holy Spirit, there are times when their use can really speak to people and add to the sense of God's presence.

I strongly recommend that you offer training for people who want to have a go, so that flags and ribbons can be used safely, thoughtfully and powerfully. We have had Saturdays when we have run worship workshops where we have just played recorded music and given people a chance to try as many different kinds of aids to worship as they want. Flagging, dancing, singing, signing, drumming, painting, listening, modelling, lying down, kneeling – all these can be a part of worship, and add to what can be a rich menu to choose from in an all-age meeting. I love flagging, and also love to see other men doing it with masculine power and speed. Women have taken the lead here, displaying grace and beauty, and we need to catch up. I also enjoy painting and have tried different ways of making a picture come together in a time of worship as an expression of my love for Jesus.

We have put paper along one wall and asked people to listen to a song and draw something from the song as they listen. The possibilities are endless and exciting. No time for getting bored!

c. *Words.* For some churches books are out and the congregation has looked towards the projector screen in times of worship, like facing towards Jerusalem! If the song you are using is simple or well known, try not having any words! I know it's radical, but try it. Everyone can concentrate on worship instead of trying to read the words and spot the spelling mistakes. Children under six cannot follow the words anyway. They learn them by heart.

d. *Repetition.* You may be part of the 'sing it only once' tradition, in which case this is not for you! In all-age meetings, it is not helpful to sing songs over too many times. Children will lose interest and drop out. However, singing a song twice can help everyone to learn the words. Don't let times of worship run too long.

3. Work out how you are going to communicate the message

It has been said that a person can concentrate for as many minutes as they have years of life. This is quite a good guideline for children's workers, but I am not sure it works once you are over eighty years old. Suffice to say each part of an all-age meeting needs to be reasonably short.

If you are going to use a story, separate it from the application, and make sure the application is as visual and exciting as the story.

Ideally the message needs to be woven through the whole meeting, so that people build on what they are learning as they go on. Try to make one point well, rather than having a six-point sermon.

People remember far more of what they see *and* hear than of what they just hear. This means that visual aids of some kind will help people to concentrate better during the meeting, and to remember better afterwards.

People remember even more if they do something related to the theme, so we almost always include some interaction where people can chat in a small group, pray for someone else, make something, find something, search in the Bible for something, or write something down. These small-group times help people to engage in the service, and they are much more likely to remember the theme at lunchtime.

Activity can also happen in other ways. One Sunday recently we used 'Blame' as our theme, and looked at how Jesus took the blame for us on the cross. We had a big plain wooden cross at the front and invited anyone to take a piece of red wool and tie it to the cross. The wool represented our blame. This kind of exercise can be very moving, and it has the effect of putting everyone in the same boat. Children, parents, single people, grandparents – all came and tied their piece of wool to the cross until it was covered in red.

At other times we have had a big dustbin, and we have invited people to come and write down things they want to say sorry for, scrunch it up, and put it in the bin. After the meeting they are all thrown away.

On another occasion we used the theme of 'the Promised Land'. In our story we learned that the priests had gathered rocks from the bed of the Jordan when God's people had crossed into the land of Canaan. They built them into an altar, as a way of showing that with God's help they were embarking on a new life, and as a declaration to the people who lived there, that this was God's land. We had enough stones at the front for everyone. Anyone who wanted could come and pick one up and place it onto a pile. They did this to show that they wanted to move forward together in their walk with God.

The Bible is full of symbolism like this, so it is not too hard to find ideas for activity. At our last Sunday service we felt that God's presence was such that we should invite people to take their shoes off. We felt we were standing on holy ground. One by one people slipped their shoes off and knelt in God's presence, children and adults together.

It takes time to introduce people to the idea of doing things in services other than standing, sitting or kneeling. Once people get used to it though, the impact of what God is saying, and the impact of their response, is experienced much more deeply, and is more likely to take root and affect their lives beyond Sunday morning. For adults to do this will often mean humbling themselves and becoming like a child!

We have taken this idea a step further with interactive worship meetings. For these, we have set up about ten or twelve worship stations around the edge of our sanctuary. At each station there is something to see and read, and a theme. There is also something to do that provides a way for the participant to express what they feel towards God. For example, we have built a huge throne from 'Quadro' (excellent resource for building worship and prayer stations!). Beside the throne we have put a craft table with all the materials for making a crown. People can write a worship prayer on the inside of the crown. When it is made they can place it at the foot of the throne. This has been a very moving exercise, and looks wonderful with dozens of golden crowns around it by the end of the morning or evening. The visual experience draws a sense of worship from those who see it, even before they begin to make their crown.

When people arrive, we usually start off with a little bit of corporate worship and an explanation of the overall theme. We also introduce everybody to the worship stations, and tell them what they can do when they visit them. After a short time we allow people to walk around and visit the stations in whichever order they choose. There are a number of advantages in doing this over a traditional all-age service: families and friends can go together; parents take time to explain spiritual truths to their children. This lays a good foundation for family prayer and worship times at home.

This kind of meeting provides lots for children to see and do. When we plan them we try to make sure there is something to stimulate all five of the senses. Children find the whole experience is an adventure.

We also provide areas for those who do not want to move around. A lounge area for people just to sit and relax – a slide show, with suitable Bible verses for people just to sit and watch.

Once the first short time, when everyone is together, has finished, people can stay or go whenever they like. Families with younger children may leave after twenty or thirty minutes, but others stay for hours, just soaking up the presence of God. Sometimes people have fallen asleep, with quiet music and a restful atmosphere to relax in.

One day a man came in from the street, and loved the peaceful environment so much, he just sat with his back against the wall. We had built a special inner sanctuary, all white with lilies and a Bible open at the Song of Solomon. A single candle was placed on a small table covered in gold material. Our visitor felt in need of a cigarette half way through the evening, and we were a little bit surprised when he decided to light up using the candle in our special 'holy place'!

4. Take truth out of the Bible and put it into today

As you build up a programme for your all-age meeting, find ways of reinforcing the message you want to get over. One of the challenges we need to overcome is to make sure that what we teach is completely relevant to today. Telling the story of Balaam's ass to show that God speaks in peculiar ways is great, but when you come to your application you need to talk about how God talks to us now. How will people hear God's voice at school and at work on Monday morning? There are a number of ways in which you can make this fun:

Drama. Tried and tested. It can work well. Write a sketch about God talking to people today. Drama works well as long as it is done to a good standard so that people can hear and understand the message. This is something that your children can get involved in, but make sure it is well practised and get those who are speaking to use microphones.

Puppets. Camilla the Camel and I have spent many hours together in schools and churches. She can magically adapt her age to the age of her listeners, and we chat about what has happened to her in the classroom, or at home. Whatever the theme, you can be sure that something has happened to her that exactly fits in. This week in infant schools we have being doing the story of Jonah, with the theme of 'saying sorry'. Camilla has been in trouble at school for purposely tripping her friend up in the playground. She knew there was a special word she needed to use if she was to make friends again, but couldn't remember what it was. The children had to shout it out for her.

I use my puppet either to introduce the theme, as in the saying sorry sketch, or sometimes at the end of a programme to reinforce the message, and to help apply it.

There are many different ways of using puppets. A puppet theatre is a great asset for all-age meetings, and again, children can team up with adults to learn how to use them.

Quizzes. School Parent/Teacher Associations have discovered that quizzes are great entertainment. They are also a great success in the local pub! I recommend them for an all-age meeting too. Apart from being great fun, they are a way to revise the main elements of the meeting, and can be used in the early part of a meeting to teach. Whenever the answer is given people learn something if they did not know the right answer before. They can also be used to help people learn general truths about the Bible, like how the books of the Bible fit together, and the overall history of God's people.

If you have a quiz, keep it short, use easy questions, and above all be seen to be completely fair. Don't favour the losing team. Children hate what they see to be injustice.

5. Prayer

I will never forget the little boy a few rows behind me who broke the heavy silence that accompanied a gentleman who was droning on and on in prayer once. He sighed deeply and said in a deafening whisper, 'Mummy, when's he going to stop?'

It is a sad thing that we have made prayer so religious and boring, and in the process it has become inaccessible to many children. It is time to rediscover the joy of talking with God, but if we are to do so, we will need to be creative, and to break down some man-made traditions. Looks like we're about to juggle another hot potato!

My first question is, why do we ask children to close their eyes when we pray? I know the official answer – it helps people to concentrate on God. But I don't think it does. Was it just me, or did other children do everything possible to keep their eyes open without being detected. I would cover my face with my hands and peek through my fingers. I would nearly close my eyes but could still see through the tiny slit I left open. I would bow my head and gaze at the carpet trying to make the patterns overlap 'magic eye' style, before magic eye had been invented! I'm sure whoever thought of magic eye pictures got the idea in a prayer meeting! If I couldn't get away with it my eyelids would quiver and I would have to screw up my face to keep them shut, but concentrate on God, I did not! Strangely enough there is no mention of closing your eyes to pray in the

Bible. There is throwing yourself face down on the ground, kneeling, raising your hands towards heaven, lifting your face towards heaven, but not closing your eyes.

I concede that I am overstating the point, and that there are times when closing your eyes is appropriate, but as a general rule it can be unhelpful for children. It is better for them to look at the person for whom they are praying, or at the person who is praying. Sometimes it can be helpful to have something as a visual focus, like a picture or an object. While it is important that everyone understands that they are not praying to the object, having a visual focus can be a way of helping people to concentrate.

My second question is, have we forgotten that God can read? There are many ways to address God other than just saying a prayer. Prayers can be written, drawn, thought, or even expressed in dance.

I love the story of King Hezekiah, whose city, Jerusalem, was surrounded by the powerful Sennacherib and his Assyrian army. Sennacherib sent a letter to Hezekiah condemning him and insulting the Lord. Note how Hezekiah responded: *'Hezekiah received the letter from the messengers and read it. Then he went up to the temple of the Lord and spread it out before the Lord'* (2 Kings 19:14). Hezekiah showed God the letter as if to let him read it himself. Writing a prayer can be very special. It is a way of expressing our pain in times of sadness, our joy and gratefulness in times of happiness, our commitment when we have decided to make a change in our lives. By writing it down, it somehow has more weight in our own minds. It can be a great way of confessing our wrongs, and when God has seen us write them, and we have asked for forgiveness, we can throw them away and begin to feel the benefit of God's forgiveness; the God who buries our sin in the deepest sea. Writing a prayer can also be more fun, and it is a way of getting everyone to pray individually.

With a young congregation like ours (15 per cent under five), we are always looking for simple things to do. Many of our children can't write, so sometimes we have used drawing as a way of praying. One word can be written on the top of a piece of paper, and drawings can be done to fit in with the word. 'Thank you', 'please' and 'sorry' are three of the most used words for this exercise.

Sometimes we use a prayer phrase like 'God you are . . .' We tell everyone what the prayer phrase will be, and give people time to think of what word or words they will choose to finish the phrase. Then the phrase is read from the front and everyone speaks out their contribution at the same time. From this we can teach that God can hear many voices at once. Other phrases we have used are; 'Jesus you are . . . ', 'Thank you God for . . . ', 'Jesus, to me your cross means . . . ', 'Jesus, to me your resurrection means . . . ', 'God I pray for . . . who needs you today', 'God please bless . . . ', 'I'm sorry for when I . . . '. The prayer phrase could be photocopied onto enough sheets for everyone to have one. Once people have written their contribution the prayers could be folded into paper planes and flown into the air. Everyone picks one plane up and everyone in the congregation reads someone else's prayer.

Prayer stations can also be used. They are very much like the worship stations we have already discussed, but have the purpose of enabling people to pray. Each station is represented by a poster, or an object, and people can walk around and choose which station to pray at. We adopted this idea some years ago. Although people find it hard to get used to the idea of walking to a place of their choice to pray, the fact that there is moving about and choice makes it more fun, and gives parents and guardians a chance to talk with their children about who or what they are going to pray for. We have had about twelve stations including; Youth, Children, The Lost, Family, The Schools, The Sick, A Map of Sheffield,

Church, The World, Unity Between Churches, The Inner City, Revival, A Union Jack, St George's Flag, and several others. They are all things that our church is concerned about. Sometimes people are encouraged to say a prayer out loud or silently, sometimes there are pens and paper for people to write prayers.

Another dimension to prayer is listening to God. Prayer isn't talking at God. It is not even talking to God. It is talking *with* God. Sometimes we make space to just listen to what we think God is saying or wants us to know. A picture or video may help as a visual focus, or some dance or mime. Music can be played for people to listen to, but the key thing is to ask people to open their hearts and minds to God. Children love to draw or write what they think God is saying, and then after a few minutes some people can be invited to share what they think God is saying. This has often been an encouragement to the church, and quite often someone will share something which unbeknown to them is a word from God to another individual.

On at least one occasion we have left our building and gone into the town for a prayer walk. The possibilities are almost endless, but all these things go beyond the 'eyes closed, hands together' approach that children find boring. They are learning to try new things in the company of the adults. They are being trained and not just taught.

6. The Notices!

You thought we would get away without them, didn't you? Sorry, but usually they are needed. They don't have to be boring though! It is important that everyone, including the children, has an idea of what is going on in the church, and of any news or prayer points that have to do with people who are a part of the body.

Camilla has often helped me when I have had to do the notices. If she is not available, it is still more fun to have two people chatting about the notices, than one person reading them solemnly. People remember them better if they are fun too. The key is that they are presented by someone who is a good all-age communicator, and that they are short. The dynamics of a wonderful all-age meeting can be killed by the notices, and the children are climbing the walls by the time they grind to a finish. If there is information specific to the grown-ups put it on the screen as people are coming in or give them a notice sheet, but don't kill the meeting by reading them out. We have even done our notices as a quiz before. It is fun to see how many people have taken in the details from their notice sheet!

7. Response

When I was at Bible College our homiletics lecturer told us that in preparation for a sermon we should always ask ourselves; 'What do I want these people to do?' This is a good question to keep in mind when planning an all-age meeting. The meeting is not an end in itself, as with any occasion when God's people meet together, it should affect the week ahead, and challenge us all to make changes that really will impact our lives.

People need to have the chance to respond in some way while they are still together. This will happen in many different ways depending on what your church is used to. People may need thirty seconds to reflect quietly, though this may not work well if you have a lot of young children around. It may be appropriate to ask people to take two minutes to chat with their household or the people they are sitting closest to about what God has said to them. As a friend of mine often says: 'Expression deepens the impression.' It might be best to call people to the front at the end of the meeting where someone can pray for them individually.

Sometimes it will help people to take something home to remind them of what God has been saying. A bookmark with a key verse written on it, a feather, a leaf or a stone. We have a number of strange objects in our house that remind us of things that God has said to us over the years.

In planning for people to respond, we need to give simple, clear, practical and achievable ideas that children and adults can put into practice. This is a bit like Jesus sending out his disciples in pairs. It is also good to give regular opportunities for people to give testimonies of what has happened as people have sought to put God's word into practice.

So there we have it. The principles are in place; the programme is coming together. There is space for items other than those we have identified as being the core items. What about an all-age Communion meeting? What about an all-age missionary service? Phone your missionary up in the middle of the meeting. It will be great fun for everyone except your poor missionary who will probably be woken up in the middle of the night!

Guidelines for parents

For an all-age meeting to work well, it will help to step back and review what you are doing from time to time. A parents' evening will give people a chance to say what they feel the hits and misses are, and to give guidelines to help parents engage their children in the meeting. These are the guidelines we use:

DO bring things that will help your child engage in the service, such as:

- Instruments (of an appropriate volume!). These will need to be carefully overseen by parents. As Ecclesiastes 3:7 says '*There is . . . a time to be silent.*' Remind children to ask before they use someone else's.

- Notebook/Paper and Pencils/Pens/Felt tips etc.:
    Suggest things your child can draw, coming out of the story or talk.

Encourage your child to write down questions coming out of the talk. They can hold a family quiz at lunch-time!

Encourage your child to write down the main points of the message.

Encourage your child to write or draw what they think God is saying to them through the message.

- Bible. Encourage your child to bring their own Bible or Bible Storybook. Help the child to find the story or passage and to follow readings.

DON'T let your child bring toys that have nothing to do with the meeting and will cause a distraction to them and others.

DO sit with your children as near to the front as possible. Get on their level if you can.

DO keep your child with you all the way through the service. Don't assume someone else is caring for them unless you have asked them to.

DO train your child to move in the parts of the service where movement is encouraged.

DO train your child to sit quietly when someone is speaking.

DO worship with your child in your arms (when they are small enough to do this). They will learn something about your intimacy with God.

DO be *'child-like'* (Matthew 18:3) in the way you worship, pray and take part. Children learn by copying.

DO interact with your children. If they do not understand what is being said, or what is happening, explain it to them quietly then and there.

DO move to the back if your child becomes unsettled, but come back to the front when and if you can.

DO come with your child for prayer or ministry at the end of the meeting if you or they would like prayer.

DO talk to your children at home about what God has been saying in the meeting.

Do feed back your comments or suggestions for improvement to the All-age Service planning group.

Just one last question

Is Sunday the best day to do it?

This could be the subject for another chapter! But here are a few brief comments.

If we want to make our all-age services accessible for people who do not regularly come to church, Sunday mornings is one of the worst times to do it. Many families see this as a day to rest. (Hey, wait a minute, isn't that a biblical idea!?) Parents do not want to get up and struggle to get children ready to go to a meeting.

Children from broken homes often go to visit the parent they are not living with on a Sunday.

Families want to spend time together, and often go out for the day.

We have found that it can be more effective to run an all-age service early evening in the middle of the week.

We do this once a month, on a Thursday evening, and use all the principles outlined in this chapter. To add a bit more of a sense of occasion we call it 'The Oaks Family House Party'. People arrive for food at 6pm (in the summer this is a barbeque). At 6.30pm we run a tightly scheduled 60-minute programme, in a TV variety programme style. To make it more authentic we have a set with easy chairs, a presenter instead of a meeting leader, and we nearly always include an episode of Pingu (a penguin cartoon family). Although the presentation style is different, the contents still include all the elements of an all age-service. Because the timing is exactly the same as our weekly midweek club (which is replaced by our house party once a month), the gap between stepping stones is not too wide, and we are picking up families who would not come to church on a Sunday morning.

Chapter 9

Dare to Dream

Raise up an army, Lord,
small in years, but large in courage,
meek in the world's eyes
but terrifying to the enemy,
armed against a spiritual foe;
misunderstood but marked with destiny.
A generation with hope, fit for revival,
unafraid, undaunted, unswerving, invincible;
like none seen on earth before.

Let them rise like the dawn,
a new day, unending;
the day of vengeance of our God.
Let the morning light dance on their armour,
let the enemy melt with fear;
worship ordained
to silence the foe and the avenger;
armed with nothing more
than the powerful love of their King.

Let them bring liberation, Lord,
to a generation under occupation,
condemned by former generations
but loved by the Saviour.
Let their hands, strong in battle

> be stronger still to rescue;
> outrageously stealing from the enemy's camp,
> plundering his prison cells,
> treading on the serpent's head.
>
> Let me see it, Lord,
> with my own eyes;
> my heart longs for you to come.
> Don't hold back;
> while some die without you,
> raise up an army, Lord,
> small in years but large in courage,
> meek in the world's eyes,
> but terrifying to the enemy.

My seat in front of the telly is a place where sometimes I cry. I have learned that crying can be a prayer in itself. We live in a world where children are so often the innocent victims of war, famine, disease, poverty, neglect, and even wilful violence. How often does the story of another abducted or murdered child rise and fade in the media. What worries me is that sometimes I don't cry! I find myself beginning to get used to the trail of tragedies in young lives, and hardened against the shock of them.

God is not like me. His heart breaks every time.

Recent years have taken me several times to the AIDS-ravaged parts of Africa. The horror of whole communities being wiped out is almost too much to grasp. The terrifying statistics show that huge proportions of the new generation are sentenced to die in the next ten years.

In our own nation children are being born with less prospect of meeting Jesus than in any generation before them.

October was a ritual for me for many years, as we got ready for our annual holiday club. 1996 was an Olympic year so our theme was Going for Gold. I bought some flags to decorate the building, and we set up a winners' podium at the front.

We used two Union flags and a St George's flag to drape slightly unrealistically above first, second and third place. On the first morning I came down early to savour the calm before the storm and to prepare a little thought for the day for the intrepid volunteers who were part of the team. The St George's flag stood out as I walked in, and I felt God was speaking to me about it. There it was – a red cross on a white background. The cross seemed to be in the right place, hanging proudly at the front, in the middle. I realised that the English flag has the cross as its main symbol, and yet its influence to all intents and purposes is fading in our country. What symbol would be chosen now, if a new flag were designed for the English? As I looked, it was as if the cross was fading, and I felt God was asking me, 'What is left, when the cross is gone?' Without the cross our flag would be a plain white flag. The flag of surrender.

As a nation we seem to carry an arrogance with us that is left over from 'winning' the war. It shows itself at football tournaments, and on foreign holiday beaches, but I wonder if we will need to face the humbling of surrender before we will turn back to God.

Any amount of legislation and policing will not change people's hearts, or stop the next appalling murder of an innocent child. Only the love of Jesus can do that. Only the re-establishment of the cross, and the humility that it brings, can make a difference.

Now I often carry that St George's flag around with me. It helps to concentrate my prayers. I have cried many tears into it. Someone once asked me if it was my comfort blanket.

Next Sunday there will be 1000 fewer opportunities to win children for Jesus in our churches than last Sunday. We need to change what we are doing if we are going to start to make a difference.

But there is hope.

In January, as God would have it, I was with my dad on the Sunday before he died, and worshipped with him in his home church that he loved so much. It was the anniversary of his joining God's family just seventy-two years previously, and Dad was not one to miss the opportunity to share his testimony. He acknowledged God's goodness in his life, and commented on the state of our nation today. Dad had grown passionate about the prospect of revival in the last few years of his life. The last thing he said as he stood to share his 'little word' was: 'What hope do we have, if God does not send revival?'

At many times in the past God has stepped in to turn a nation upside down. Often this has followed many years of prayer for revival. A child has often been the spark that God has used to set things off.

Sadly, prayer for revival is sometimes seen as the domain of one section of the church. Whether we use the word revival or not, surely anyone who loves Jesus has an aching longing to see the kingdom of God established in their own land, and for a return to godly values and principles that will make us a truly great nation. It is time for patriotism based on compassion and humility, instead of selfishness and pride.

I get excited every time I read some new story of God at work in the world. In contrast to the UK, the church is growing like wildfire around the world. Europe is the only continent not experiencing revival in the early twenty-first century, and there are more Christians alive today than the sum of all those who have died.

My prayer is 'Lord, we are desperate for you to do it here, in our time, and among our children.'

In this last chapter I want to share a few of the stories that have blessed me. I hope they will encourage you, and give us all a greater expectation of what God can do among children. I have also invited some young people to write down their vision for the future.

This first story is set in Cincinnati, from the diary of Lynne Hammonds in 1885. She visited Woodworth and began to pray with five of the leaders in a small Methodist church, which she describes as 'cold and formal'.

The class leader's little boy fell under the power of God first. He rose up, stepped on the pulpit, and began to talk with the wisdom and power of God. His father began to shout and praise the Lord. As the little fellow exhorted and asked the people to come to Christ they began to weep all over the house. Some shouted, others fell prostrated. Divers operations of the Spirit were seen. The displays of the power of God continued to increase till we closed the meetings, which lasted about five weeks. The power of the Lord like the wind, swept all over the city, up one street and down another, sweeping through the places of business, the workshops, saloons and dives, arresting sinners of all classes . . . Men, women and children were struck down in their homes, in their places of business, on the highways, and lay as dead. They had wonderful visions, and rose converted, giving glory to God. When they told what they had seen, their faces shone like angels. The fear of God fell on the city. There was no fighting, no swearing on the street; that the people moved softly, and that there seemed to be a spirit of love and kindness among all classes, as if they felt they were in the presence of God.

A merchant fell in a trance in his home and lay several hours. Hundreds went in to look at him. He had a vision and a message for the church. The Lord showed him the condition of many of the members. He told part of his vision, but refused to deliver the message to the church. He was struck dumb. He could not speak a word because he refused to tell what the Lord wanted him to. The Lord showed him he would never speak till he delivered the message. He rose to his feet weeping to tell the vision. God loosed his tongue. Those present knew he had been dumb, and when he began to talk and tell his experience it had a wonderful effect on the church and on sinners.

The people came to the meetings in sleigh loads from many miles. One night when they were jesting about trances, they made the remark to each other that they were going in a trance that night. Before the meeting closed all that had been making fun were struck down by the power of God and lay like dead people, and had to be taken home in the sled in that condition. Those that came with them were very much frightened when they saw them lying there and they told how they had been making fun of the power of God on the way to the meeting. Scoffers and mockers were stricken down in all parts of the house.

One man was mocking a woman whose body God had taken control. She was preaching with gestures, when in that mocking attitude God struck him dumb. He became rigid and remained with his hands up, and his mouth drawn in that mocking way for five hours, a gazing stock for all in the house. The fear of God fell on all. They saw it was a fearful thing to mock God or to make fun of his work. Surely the Lord worked in a wonderful way at this meeting. The *Cincinnati Enquirer* sent a reporter to write up the meetings and report daily. Every day the newsboys could be heard crying out 'All about the Woodworth Revival'. Reporters came from many states and large cities to write up the meetings.

This is a story not so much about children in revival, as revival sparked by the words of a child. Oh that the new generation would be a righteous voice to our nation. Can God bring revival through a child again?

This next story is geographically closer to home. It is the story of children affected by revival, and how their example affected the adults who came to watch. I can still hear the words of Jesus as I read this account. *'See that you do not look down on one of these little ones'* (Matthew 18:10).

A loft in Belfast in 1859.

A clergyman arrived to find the steps crowded with children, and he helped some of them up. A mother who saw him exclaimed: 'Oh no, here's a minister! He'll stop the wee ones.' But he assured her that he had come to learn. She told him that the meeting had been going on every evening for two months, from 7.30pm till 10pm. The oldest of the leaders was thirteen.

The minister counted 48 children squatting on the floor, eager and reverent. When one of the candles fell on the boy's head and singed his hair, there was no stir, not even a titter; he quietly picked it up and put it back.

At the far end of the loft were benches occupied by 70-80 adults, but it was the children who led. The leader was a boy of thirteen, who prayed with power and conviction: 'Show us our mountain of sin, so that we can feel that you are our Saviour from them. Though we are slaves to Satan, yet you, Jesus, can set us free forever! Loose the bonds of sin, O Jesus our deliverer! O Lord, teach us truth and purity. Search all our thoughts, examine our hearts, show us all the things that are hateful in your sight! We pray you to burn out all our inmost sins and wicked thoughts, against you, and against each other. Burn them out, O pure Jesus, but save us in the burning.'

A boy of twelve then tried to teach from Matthew's Gospel, but got stuck on the long words, so exhorted instead: 'Won't you come to Jesus and get baptised in the Spirit? O come away from the Devil and come for Jesus! Prepare the way of the Lord! How many of you are in Hell? You know you don't feel free from the Devil. Jesus wants to come for you.'

And so it continued, the boys speaking one by one in orderly fashion. One needed practical help. His parents could not afford to pay the next week's rent. The children all got out their pocket money and the sum was met.

Then the clergyman got a shock because the girls began to pray. This offended his traditions, but he let the Spirit move. A girl of seventeen prayed fervently for the conversion of her family and for forgiveness for all her ingratitude to God. Another much younger declared: 'I do love Jesus, and I'm not afraid to say what a Saviour I've found!'

Then a small girl of about ten arose, frail in body, and clothed with rags. Trembling with the Lord's anointing, she raised her hand and proclaimed Jesus crucified for our sins. The power fell instantly. A teenage boy slumped to the floor. Many began to weep. Two or three twelve-year-olds lay prostrate on the floor. Cries filled the air: 'Mercy Jesus, can you save me? Help! I'm finished!' Others felt the touch of God's mercy and sang loud praises; tears streaming down their beaming faces.

Finally, well past ten o'clock, the gathering ended with a favourite hymn, 'Ye sleeping souls arise', and a very inspired clergyman returned to his hotel praising the Lord.

In August each year for ten years we ran a camp in Scarborough for children aged nine to twelve. Camp 1994 turned out to be a very special year for us, as God moved in great power among the children. This is an extract from an account I wrote three years later, based on my own diary from the time:

On Wednesday, 17 August, John O'Brien had been speaking. At the end of the meeting I had a picture in my mind of a fuel tank, with the needle on empty. I shared this, and invited children to stay if they wanted to be filled up by the Holy Spirit. About twelve stayed behind. I remember that it was very quiet. As we began to pray, the sense of God's

Spirit became stronger than I have ever known before. Quietly one child after another seemed overcome. Some were lowered to the floor and lay peacefully for up to half an hour. Some just stood with tears running down their cheeks. Others wanted to tell God they were sorry for being away from him. I remember one boy wearing big fluffy hedgehog slippers lying quite still, both hedgehogs with their noses pointing heavenwards. As the week went by, many of the leaders were deeply affected by what God was doing. There was practically no noise, just a deep sense of God's presence.

During the rest of the week God continued to work very powerfully. Nineteen children said that they wanted to become Christians. Children who themselves had been touched by God wanted to pray for each other and the leaders. The same things were happening to the leaders, as to the children. Meetings finished with children staying for up to an hour – often missing tuck-shop or an evening drink, preferring to stay where God's presence could be felt.

Two or more leaders watched over these ministry times at the end of each meeting, not leaving until the last child left, or was carried up to bed. For the first time in fifteen years I found tears welling up in my own eyes as I watched what God was doing. I cannot put into words the way I felt.

For the rest of the week, each meeting seemed touched by God in a special way. There were many tears, both from leaders and children. Tears of repentance, joy, and a concern for friends and relatives who did not know Jesus. Extra tissues, and a lot of toilet rolls were used to blow noses and dry eyes.

Subsequent years have continued to see children touched deeply by the presence of God. On a number of occasions we have had evenings when we have turned the focus outwards, and have prayed for revival. I will never forget the sight of children kneeling below the St George's flag praying tearfully for mercy for our country, and for revival, or of children pleading with God for the salvation of their families and friends.

Can God bring revival through the prayers of a child?

Can God bring revival to our schools? It has happened before.

Baptist minister Harry Sprange has collected a remarkable catalogue of stories of children in revival from Scotland over the last three hundred years. This account is taken from his book *Children in Revival.*

The story is set in Pilrig, Edinburgh, and commences with the conversion, following a mission led by Finney, of headmaster William Robertson on the 10 August 1859, the same year as the Belfast story. The following day, the headmaster led his deputy to the Lord, and a week later they prayed together for the six oldest children in the school to be saved. In Robertson's own words:

The work of that morning went on much the usual way with this exception. During the Bible lesson, one girl, usually very thoughtless, was rather trifling, talking continuously to her neighbour. She was removed to another seat, and went quite readily. After some time, she began to cry. I did not think anything of this, but after the lesson was finished, and when all the other children had gone to the playground for a few minutes, she continued in her seat still crying. When I asked her what was the matter, she answered that it was for her sins.

The girl was not one of those we had prayed for . . . during the rest of the forenoon she sat in her class evidently quite unable to take any part in the work. She sat with her hands clasped, from time to time heaving a deep sigh. But speaking to no one. She requested that at the prayer meeting they should sing Psalm 16:1-4, which they did. At one o'clock the schoolwork was resumed for the afternoon. The highest class had a writing lesson. Copybooks and pens had been distributed, and work was beginning when I noticed a girl crying. She was seated at the end of one of the seats. On my asking what was wrong she answered that it was her sins. Just then the teacher came up to me and told me that a great number more were crying; he wished to know what he should do with them. I told him to show them into the classroom. Those girls for whom we had been praying that morning came in one by one, crying most bitterly. Oh the solemnity and the awfulness of that moment, I never shall forget. God was manifestly in our midst in awakening power, answering prayer. The lad prayed for was also awakened that day . . . After these five girls had entered the room, there was a pause as if the Lord would have us notice how he had heard our cry and was answering our morning prayer. Shortly after, another eight boys and girls came in and took their seats beside their companions. They sang a hymn, and he spoke briefly to them.

There was an intelligent girl, Katie B. sitting at the end of a seat, and as she was nearest to me I said to her, 'Katie, could you not trust Jesus?' quoting some of our Saviour's own most gracious words. She looked up into my face, her large bright eyes filling with tears, and answered, 'Yes, sir, I could trust Jesus,' and then starting to her feet she began to speak to her companions, naming them, 'Oh Hannah, could you not trust Jesus?', 'Jemima, could you not trust Jesus?', quoting some of our Lord's words.

Her companions looked up in astonishment at her, and as she went on telling them of Jesus and his power to save, I saw that the Lord was himself guiding and teaching this dear girl. I thus left her with her companions and returned to the school-room. Here I found all the children in tears, everyone without exception, and the assistant doing his best among them. Telling them of Jesus. I did not imagine they were all anxious; some of the younger children were crying, no doubt, out of sympathy with their elder brothers and sisters. I went to the youngest class, saying that this would never do, or words to that effect. Some of them took out their books to begin work, but others looked into my face and burst out afresh into weeping. It was quite evident that all work was impossible for that afternoon. Accordingly we brought all the children together into the larger schoolroom, locating them in a gallery gradually rising from the floor. There would be about ninety altogether in this department. They were all together in this gallery, and all of them either crying or with their faces showing traces of tears. I should have said that earlier in the afternoon, when the feeling was greatest, I had sent a boy to fetch Mr Blakie. He had returned from the Manse with the message that Mr Blakie was not at home, but that as soon as he had come home he would come along to the school.

Just as we had gathered the children into the gallery, the former Superintendent of the Sabbath

School paid us a visit. It was long since he had promised us this visit, and it so happened that at this moment he arrived. He was naturally very much astonished at what he saw, and on his inquiring as to what was the matter, I invited him to apply to the children themselves. Our visitor did so, and on applying to a boy near him he got for answer that his sins were the cause of trouble. With reference to this boy spoken to, the teacher afterwards told me that shortly before, when he had seen his cousin, a girl of thirteen, crying, he had made fun of her, calling her a baby and so forth. He had asked her what was wrong, and in reply she had exclaimed, 'Oh, Frankie, it's my sins.' In a few minutes he sat down beside her and seemed as much distressed as any.

After having spoken to this boy, our visitor asked if they were all in the same state of mind. I replied that they all said so when asked. Later on I remarked that surely the Lord had sent him in to visit at that moment, and invited him to say a few words to the children. He did so, but was too much overcome to say much.

The work of this revival continued in the days that followed with more children coming to a saving knowledge of Jesus on the following Tuesday. It is also exciting to read about the effect the children had on their families.

The mother of Jeannie, the first girl awakened, came to Mr Robertson to ask what he had done to her daughter, who usually lost her temper if her dinner wasn't ready when she got home, but just sat quietly by the fire sighing. Jeannie's sister and Mr Robertson prayed together after school one day for the mother's conversion, and later this woman, a drunkard, was converted. Mr Robertson picks up the story:

> As I was leaving Free St Luke's church one day, the father of two girls in Pilrig School accosted me, anxious to speak about them. He had been much annoyed, he said, by his girls singing hymns at home, and at length, after some time he had forbidden them to do so, at least while he was in the house. The girls had been greatly disturbed about this, as was also their mother, but, concluding that their father only wished not to hear them singing, they continued the singing after they had gone to bed, covering their heads with the blankets. He heard them singing, however, and an arrow of conviction entered his heart. It was in great distress of soul that he had come to me saying, 'My girls will be on the right side of the throne and I will be on the left. I never taught them to pray. Is there any hope for a sinner like me?'
>
> It was a great joy to point this awakened father to the Lord Jesus as his Saviour, and to show him that there was certainly forgiveness for him. We can only imagine the joy of these two girls, when they learned that their father also was trusting in their precious Saviour.

Children in Revival records several more fascinating stories about the faith of the children from the Pilrig School revival: friends who were brought to Jesus, a child who died knowing him. The book also recounts other times and places when awakening swept through whole schools and touched local communities.

So much for the past. Is there any spark of spiritual life in the new generation today?

A passion, determination and devotion is rising up in the new generation, that brings hope for the twelve million young people living in the UK.

Sometimes I have cried in church. But this time the tears are tears of hope and joy. They have flowed as I have listened to children and teenagers preaching with a passion for Jesus that I never had when I was their age. I have cried as I have listened to the desperate plea from a teenager for the church to pray for her friends at school. This same girl arranged to hand out a gospel leaflet to every young person in her year one Easter. The tears have flowed as I have watched discipled young people rising up to lead worship with a passion that puts my faith to shame. I have watched as a fourteen-year-old has set about the task of raising funds to go on a short-term mission overseas. Prayer groups are springing up in our schools, initiated and run entirely by Christian pupils. Children at infant school are prayer walking their playgrounds at break time. Children are believing that following Jesus can be a glorious adventure. Jesus said: *'I will build my church, and the gates of hell will not prevail against it'* (Matthew 16:18). Hope outweighs despair!

A number of prayer movements are rising up across our nation. One of these is J2 (from Joel chapter 2:16) founded by John and Maria O'Brien. J2 is simply an environment where the new generation can rise up and pray. Each time I have watched as a sense of destiny and purpose has swept in powerfully across the young people present. They have wept and worshipped, danced and declared, repented and recommitted themselves to serving Jesus. There has been a great cry from their hearts for their own generation. It is time for my generation to disciple, and then step back and let the new generation have a voice. I have asked two of them to put into a few words what is in their hearts for the future, for themselves, and for the generation they represent:

I'm 17, and studying A levels at school.

What breaks my heart is to see the friends who I love and have grown up with, looking for love in all the wrong places. If only they knew what God thinks of them, and how precious they are in his eyes. I cry for them, pray for them in desperation that they will encounter God's presence.

I believe that nothing can compare to being in the heavenly presence of God. Sometimes I can see an image of a tiny person reaching their hand out towards heaven in worship, and this hand touching the palm of the gigantic, strong and light hand of God. If we choose to let go of our inhibitions in worship, he reaches out to us – he stretches further!

This can be such a challenge to our generation, with all our insecurities, peer pressure, and broken self-esteem. We've all been in the position where standing in church, you feel you want to cry out, raise your hands in the air, or fall on your knees, but something inside won't let you break out of your box. My vision is to see those teens, and younger ones, leading the way and working along-side anointed worship leaders. Totally forgetting themselves in God's presence, in complete surrender to the Spirit. I have such respect for the worship leaders in my church who are humble enough to let us youth be their apprentices.

Our age group can be seen as a 'problem area' because of our negative attitude and disrespect for ourselves and God, but my prayer is that this generation would become a problem for God's enemy!

Faith Reed

I was in a seminar at Grapevine, a Christian conference, when the preacher called us to open our hearts to God, asking him to give us a dream for our generation. I've always found it hard to clear my mind so I can listen to God, but this time I was able to do it. I closed my eyes and waited unexpectantly for a word. After a few moments of nothing, I suddenly saw each assembly hall in my school packed with students and teachers worshipping the Lord, and the musicians in the school leading the worship. The sight of it reduced me to tears. I have always had it on my heart for the youth of this nation to be hit by God, to realise his glory. I see this longing as a fire in my heart, often just smouldering as I am surrounded by secular life. But at moments like this, I feel the fire burning in my heart. No matter what, the fire is always there as I long to see this generation saved.

Another picture that has been strongly implanted in my mind is of a crown hovering above my school with the words 'Jesus is King' written directly above it. Looking round at the people in my school, I know they need God. I want to see my school claimed for Jesus – to shine with his light.

Maybe it seems a bit much for us to comprehend – 2000 people saved from one school, but it is by no means unheard of. I believe we need to have great expectations of God, for him to give us great things. If we know something can be done naturally, then it requires no faith, and what God requires of us is faith. Seeing is never believing, but if we believe, then we will see God work with unimaginable power in this nation.

My vision is to see the youth of this nation saved by the only one who can: Jesus Christ, the name above all names – but how many people know that?

Rachel Sutcliffe

God is speaking to and through the new generation more clearly and more powerfully than ever before, and this gives old wrinklies like me great hope, and a sense of anticipation.

But what about us? Are we to become redundant as God begins his work through young people?

There is something very powerful about seeing the walls between generations crumbling in the church. To see all ages crying out to God together to do something in our nation. I do not believe God is calling us to be John the Baptists, who must step out for the sake of letting the new generation supersede us. There is much we can do together, and there is a destiny for those who are called to work with young people that we have not yet fully realised.

The vision needs to be caught by children and youth workers, by parents, and perhaps most of all by church leaders.

Maybe together we can see revival come to our land. Maybe we are training the generation that will see Jesus return!